Margene Wiese-Baier

Angels IN FLIGHT II

DAILY INSPIRATIONS

Primix Publishing
East Brunswick Office Evolution
1 Tower Center Boulevard, Ste 1510
East Brunswick, NJ 08816
www.primixpublishing.com
Phone: 1-800-538-5788

Front Cover Angel by Artist: Marianne (Ria) Sopala
Front Cover Cloud Photo by Artist: Margene Wiese-Baier
Back Cover Photo Composition by Artist: Gerd Altman

Also, the photos are mine. No Models. P.127 is the only photo taken from the Internet. A free photo.

Published by Primix Publishing: 12/02/2024

ISBN: 979-8-89194-276-9(sc)
ISBN: 979-8-89194-277-6(e)

Library of Congress Control Number: 2024916432

PRIMIX
PUBLISHING
THE WRITE CHOICE

Angels in Flight

Genesis 28:12 (King James Version)

Daily Inspirations

Margene Wiese-Baier

Dedicated to my Mom and Dad!

Words are power and, when written down, last forever. I grew up watching my Mom write songs, poems, and novels. My heart broke when she went to Heaven before her time. Most of her works went unpublished, but she left a legacy of love for writing and a passion for art. I have found that these mingle together in perfect harmony.

She taught me at a young age about Jesus, so both my artwork and writing are inspired by the Holy Spirit. I don't believe in compromising my faith to make an impression upon people. Friendships can fade away, but His love is eternal, so I hope and pray that people can see His reflection in my words. I grew up in Oregon and where destiny has called me. My Dad is my Rock and Support.

*This book is also for my fellow brothers and sisters,
to lift you up in your daily walk with God.*

Contents

God's Bucket List
Serving Others Pays a Great Return
Renewed and Refreshed
Ask for Help
Let God Drive, You Rest Awhile
Finding Our Place

A Prayer to Share

Dear Father,

I come before You this morning with my petitions, not only for myself but for my friends and family.

Before I do that, I want to thank You for Your special gift of Jesus Christ, Your son, and all that he did for me.

I come humbly before You in my pursuit to pray happiness and health and provisions, but most of all wisdom, not only for myself, but for my family and friends.

Father, in this day, we need more than enough. Not only for ourselves, but enough that we can help our fellow man, that when someone says I need your help that we can reach into our pocket and help that person or we can provide a meal or whatever is needed. I ask for direction in how and when I am supposed to supply that need. I ask that I am the one who can direct them to where they need to go to learn how to fish to last a lifetime and not the one that just hands them enough to just last them for the day. Please, don't let me pass an opportunity to show the love of Jesus. Let Him shine through me.

Father, I ask that if I have offended anyone that they forgive me and that our relationship is mended for Your glory. I ask that I am able to forgive anyone who has offended me intentionally or unintentionally and that relationships are mended for Your glory.

Father, I ask that You bring to the forefront of my memory people I need to pray for or call them, that I do it when they come to my mind and not wait, knowing they are in need at the time and that is why I am thinking of them.

Father, I ask for divine appointments, divine opportunities, and divine connections that bring transformation in not only my life, but also to those whom I connect with for Your glory. Not that I can boast about for myself, but boast about You, and I can share with others on how good You are in my life.

I ask that You cleanse anything out of me that is not of You. I ask for protection and Your guidance in all things, big and small. I ask that I give credit where credit is due, if that is to You or someone whom You have used to bring about something good in my life. Ultimately, it all comes back to Your intervention in all that occurs in my life. I will remember Psalms 23 and 91 that have been provided for me to cover me and shield me in these days of trials and tribulation.

Father, I thank You for all of my family, and I ask that You bless them and keep them. I ask for my friends that You do the same. For the relationships that have come into my life that are truly like family to me a special double anointing, for they are the ones who truly understand who I am and who I stand for. All in all, the people whom you placed in my life were the divine appointments, the divine opportunities, and the divine connections. I ask for more people to come into my life so that I can share Your love. I thank You for the pastors, the prophets and apostles, and the evangelists and the teachers who have come into my life who have fed me Your word and that I have gotten fat on their teaching to get me ready for the things I need to do for You. I thank You that they have given me a step up into my destiny.

Most of all, I just want to thank You for who You are!

In Jesus's name, Amen and Amen.

A Little Attitude Adjustment!

Today I am thankful for the growth in myself in knowing who He is—and standing up for what I believe. Some may think I am radical, but after you almost die and see the hand of God bring you back, maybe you will understand how I can't just leave it alone. After an accident in March, I told myself I was not going to keep my faith quiet. I have accepted what others have told me and seemed to be stopped when I try to tell them about myself and what I believe.

Some might tell you that I have never been quiet in what I believe, but that is just not so. I have been to another country where people wanted to hear what I've had to say. I have a little attitude. Well, yeah. About time, huh? Okay, maybe I am only talking to myself. David talked to himself, encouraging himself. Thank you to others who know where I am coming from and to those who only wish they knew.

Apology Accepted or Rejected?

Have you ever apologized for doing something that seemed so right at the time, but to the other person, it was the wrong thing to do? Recently, I made such a judgment call, and I have been paying for it ever since.

Do you ever get so excited and zealous over a project that things just happen before you know it, and then the person you are trying to help reacts in a completely different way than expected?

Being overexcited and overly zealous is what has happened to me. I thought I was helping someone, and I did something that I thought would be an improvement and the other person saw it as a destruction. I had all these grandiose ideas how I could help this person and acted before I got called back by the other person involved. They were helping me with my situation, and I wanted to do my part by making things better for them as well. Thinking that they would see it the same way and appreciate what I had done, I acted, and they reacted—in a way I did not expect for sure.

This was a project I was trying to get done before the end of December. I am the kind of person that when I have a plan, I want to get on with it. Time restraints help me in these times. I had made contacts with people who could help me achieve my goal, and I was going for it. Full steam ahead! Let's get this done. I want to help this person, and I know how I can get the job done. Unfortunately, that person didn't realize that I had all this planned out. They just saw the tearing-down part; they didn't hear me say I had a plan to make everything right and beautiful for them. I was going to not only pour my sweat and blood into this project, but my money too.

This person saw me as every other Christian who says, "Yes, I will help you," and then doesn't follow through. I wanted to follow through, but when someone reacts in such a way, it throws me backward. I have to regroup and get everything into perspective again. I want to help this person, but they have to forgive me for not waiting for them to give me the go-ahead. I was the person who was going to be dealing with situations after everything was put back in order. I guess that is why I thought it would be okay to use my own judgment.

Life is too short to stay mad at people. Items can be replaced. Relationships are sometimes harder to repair. Don't close yourself off to the people who really do have your best interest in mind. True friends are hard to come by who really do care about you and want everything to work out for the best in your life.

Please forgive others, and for goodness' sakes, stop bringing it up. They already feel bad enough that they did what they did. Stop and think about it. Did they really do what they did to hurt you? Or did they do it because they thought they were helping you? If they tell you that they did it to help, accept it as truth because more than likely, it is the truth. People don't usually set out to intentionally hurt others, but remember, there is the enemy who is out to kill, steal, and destroy. And if he can destroy your relationship with others, then he can destroy you.

I am hoping that this person knows my heart and that I would not do anything to intentionally hurt them. Time was short, and I acted upon knowing that, and I hope that they remember that I still want to help them if they let me and if they still want my help. Just think what could have happened if their reaction would have been different. It would have been a beautiful sight.

Assuming Is the Lowest Form of Intelligence

"Assuming is the lowest form of intelligence." I got this from Pastor Quintin King, who is married to Pastor Freda, one of my mentors. They are two people whom I love dearly.

Don't just assume you are right about something unless you have all the facts. Assuming something can cause division and hurt in relationships. Sometimes we play the guessing game because we are unwilling to listen to what the other person is saying.

Still Single and Still Okay

One thing I will never understand is when friends and family are so concerned about you being single. They will send you information about men or try to hook you up with people they wouldn't even go out with. Please stop; it is upsetting and actually cruel. Let God send us our mates, and when we find someone, don't interfere. Let us make our own decisions about the person. It is our life, not yours.

Be a Star, Not a Crab in Someone's Life

I recently wrote a note that had crabs and stars in it. I was talking to a friend yesterday, and she was telling me about how one of her friends was buddy-buddy with her when she wasn't doing well, but when my friend was doing well, this would cause trouble in their friendship.

She then proceeded to tell me that at a Bible study, she heard that it is best to let people go who are causing strife in your life. You give them two chances and then let them go.

Wow, pruning time again.

I am a person who I think gives people more than two chances, but sometimes I get burnt and my feelings get hurt because I tend to love them more than they love me.

I know the Father, Son, and Holy Spirit; if they weren't forgiving, none of us would have a chance. But humans are different; He is the only one who can change that person. Try though we will, we might hit a brick wall if we try to change someone. Sometimes, we just have to let them go. Sometimes, we get hurt in the process, but we grow from the experience. He sometimes prunes us from relationships so that we will grow. As painful as it might be, we sometimes have to let certain people go out of our lives because they are poison to our very being.

For me, this has been a very hard lesson. The people I thought would be backing me are now gone out of my life for one reason or another. I've had jobs with people who promised me the moon but did not fulfil a single word they said. I've had friendships deteriorate when I did not bow to their every whim.

If the truth be known, when you make a God connection with someone, they love you and lift you up in prayer when the chips are down. They rejoice with you when you are doing well. They cry with you when you need to cry. They hold your hand when you are about to fall. They encourage you when you have had something or someone upset you. They let Jesus talk through them to help show you the way when you have no idea how to get there. Wherever there is trouble, they listen to you when they are feeling down as well and know in their heart that the Holy Spirit is talking through you in order to help guide them to the answers and wisdom they need to hear. They don't judge you when you're a little off that day. They cover your back when someone or something tries to come against you.

I could go on and on, and I know some of you could add to this list as well. I may not have met you face-to-face, but there is no distance in God. All the things I wrote above are how I feel about the people who visit my online ministry and speak with me through the words on these pages. I have personal friends, and I know that I am loved and encouraged, and we work together to bring Him glory, but I feel called to reach out and help more people with my writing and my prayers.

I hope something in here will bless you. Anything not of God disintegrates. Let us all be stars in someone's life; leave the crabs to be cooked in their own juices, they taste better that way.

Be Like the Butterfly

Butterflies always remind me of humans and the way we all have to go through something hard to get to appreciate something beautiful in our lives. As the butterfly is in the cocoon and is struggling to get out, he gets stronger and stronger as he pushes his way to freedom.

As humans, we get stronger as we keep pushing toward the goal our Father has set before us. He is right there to help pull us through to what He wants in our lives.

So don't despise those times of struggle in your life; it just means something beautiful is about to happen. I pray favor over all my friends and family who read this. God has put us together using the body of Christ to create beautiful butterflies together and to soar like eagles through the skies.

Compassion and Forgiveness

Don't be deceived by the enemy; he has come to kill, steal, and destroy.

I try to remember this when it comes to my relationships that have ended through no fault of my own, and if I have offended anyone, I ask for their forgiveness. I will admit when I am wrong, but I will not take on blame that is not mine to take. Thanksgiving is here, and Christmas is coming, and it is a time to connect with loved ones. Let's clean the slate and have compassion for one another. Just a thought.

Dance with Me, Oh Lover of My Soul

Today I am talking to those who have felt that tugging at their heart-strings to go forward and worship but have been hindered in some way. Oh, I am shy, I am quiet. I don't know how to dance. That just isn't me.

Well no, it isn't you, it is something inside of you that wants to press in and get everything that He has for you, to look up and to get into His presence and to exalt Him. I want everyone to feel the excitement that I am feeling. Can you imagine if everyone went forward in one accord? What would happen? What could happen? Wowser! Wowser! Wowser! What joy it would bring to our King, to have everyone unite in one body and give Him all the glory.

Why is it that we do not have any trouble going forward when the Pastor does an altar call for something we need or want from our Father, but it is so hard to get out of our seats to go worship Him? It saddens my heart to think that we are so self-centered. We are not just part of one church, but God is sending us out to other places. We are to bring the light; we are to bring the Worship. When we go into another church, people should notice that there is something different about us. We don't go forward to worship to say, "Look at me, I am special," but to get into His presence, to bring Him all the glory, and if we can help bring others into His presence, how cool is that?

Father, let me be the one to let Your light shine through me, a beacon that radiates your love, to give a hug and let my arms be Your arms around that person, to give a smile that radiates Your love through my lips, to lay hands on them in healing, knowing it isn't me that is doing the healing, but You working through my vessel for I am only an instrument to be used by You.

"Dance with Me, Oh Lover of My Soul." That song just keeps resonating in my mind and heart. All He asks is that you come and dance with Him. I remember when I first started going to Suncoast Worship Center, I said to God, "This is so weird." He told me to shut my eyes, and He would show me how to worship Him, to stop looking at everyone else and how they are worshiping.

The next thing I knew, I was up front dancing. At that time, there were several people dancing up front. This was in the old Sanctuary, and there were a lot of glory holes in that place. It felt like an open Heaven—such freedom. I pray that for the building that we are in now, that the chains of bondage are broken off. We sing the song freedom, but do we really have it? Are we really living it, or are we squelching the things He has for us by not obeying Him when He asks us to go forward?

Maybe some of us need a little help and encouragement from our fellow members, so we have two left feet, but God is not looking at our feet, but our heart. When we sing, it may sound to us like that person is tone-deaf, but God sees the person's heart, and it is truly beautiful to Him. It is anointed and may bring someone to worship Him also.

At our church, we use the scenario about being at a football game and yelling for our team. Why can't we make a joyful noise for our Father? In the Communion with God class, Bonnie said, "If we're willing to go to nightclubs and dance in the world, why not dance for Jesus?" Wowser, what a revelation!

I was at Deep Creek Worship Center, and God had Judy down on the floor, and HE confirmed everything I am saying here. Maybe in our younger years, we went out dancing in the world. Dancing and singing are just some of the things that are really gifts given to be used in the Church.

I am just so excited to see what God is doing in many of our lives, especially when it is happening in my own life too. There are a lot of things that are still in process, of course, but what a process! What a joy to be living in a time such as this. Wow, so awesome! I get anxious sometimes because God's timing is not my timing, but He has never failed me. The answers are not always the answers I am expecting. His ways are always better than my ways.

I can't wait to see what He does next.

Learning the Hard Way Again

Did you ever do something and find out you did it the hard way?

Why is it sometimes in life we do this and find out later that if we just took a few minutes in the first place to check things out, it would have been a lot smoother, and it would have taken half the time? Calling on our Father first always helps. He shouldn't be an afterthought.

God's Canvas

When I was a child, my Mom saw that I was an artist and directed me in that direction while she directed my sister in the direction of academics. My sister thrived on learning in school, and to this day, she still does. Now she's a teacher and so much more. I seemed to thrive in a different environment. I just learned completely different than my sister. I was an A student until I got really sick in the sixth grade, and then I seemed to have a more difficult time in school, but if I was allowed to put my artistic flair to the subject, I was able to get the good grades.

Do you understand that when you do what you were meant to do, everything falls into place? Like my sister, even though she didn't understand why she was in certain jobs, why she went to certain schools, it opened up her mind to download, as it were, the things she is doing now. Like me, I have learned that just because we do not learn the same way as each other, we can still interact and learn from each other. Embracing the differences in each other and not putting ourselves down will bring people closer together.

So the next time you see a go-getter, know that you are a go-getter too, but just not in the same way as another person might be. Check it out, look at yourself; beneath the surface, we are not that different after all, but oh, the differences can be lifesaving.

I am happy to be the King's kid. He had the plan for me before the foundations of the world and before I was formed in my mother's womb. Wow, when I look at it that way, I can say that I love that I am different and an individual, and there is no one else like me, and you can say the same thing. Let us rejoice and be glad.

When Everything Falls into Place

Do you have people in your life that no matter their age, they are go-getters? They have a passion for life and get the job done. Sometimes, we don't see the good in ourselves, but we can in other people. Or on the flip side, it occurs also. Be kind to yourself and rewind and look who you are supposed to reflect. Embrace who you are because you are the King's kids. He made you the way you are for a reason.

Sometimes I look at others and think, Wow, they get so much done. They have so many ideas. They are so smart. And I look at myself, especially when I don't feel on top of the world, and I don't feel I am accomplishing anything that I consider even close to what they are doing. I sabotage myself, forgetting that He didn't make me like them for a reason.

Then I ask myself, If we all were alike, how boring would that be? Just because my intelligence doesn't lie in the same direction as theirs, does that make me less smart? I think not.

Don't Give Up on Your Dreams

This is not the year to give up on your dreams, but to fulfill them. I, for one, have some promises I felt that were made to me that I want to see come to pass. I know I have a lot of friends and family who feel the same way for themselves. For this year, let us pray for each other for the best for each other—no more jealousy and disharmony, but genuine love and hope and joy for each other.

I have heard it said many times, if our Father can do it for you, He can do it for me. So let us join together in this journey of love and choose to hope for and truly want the best for one another. Just a thought. Hugs and many, many blessings in this year and in the many years to come.

Don't Want to Go Around This Mountain Again!

I have to be honest here. I will be glad when this year is over. I know we have to go through hard times so we can help others through their tough times, but I don't always have to like it. God didn't promise just because we are Christians that we would escape the troubles and problems of the world, but there is a reason for everything.

I guess if I look through the Bible, I see story after story of the horrific things that people went through, and God didn't desert them. Wow, He even let a big fish swallow up one guy by the name of Jonah. What a slimy experience that must have been! And then look at Joseph, his father's favorite, yet he ends up in prison (a roundabout way to get to the top for sure). Think about David—the list goes on. And then the biggest sacrifice was his son, Jesus.

Well, I guess my point is, each of these people had a destiny, but it wasn't always clear to them nor easy to accomplish, and without God's intervention, they would still be in the whale, the prison, or even on the cross. So I guess I am going through the Refiner's fire because I have something better coming. I know to everyone who knows me, it looks like I am struggling, and believe me, I am, but I have to hold to my belief that this, too, God will bring me through, and I will be able to say God had me in the palm of His hand all along.

He has used many people at the times I have needed help, and I want to thank them for being God's instruments for your music is beautiful when you've opened your heart to help someone else.

I just don't want to go around this mountain again. Remembering the times He brought me through other situations helps me to know that He will do it again and for others. If they remember this too, it will help.

Enemy, Talk to the Hand

Enemy, talk to the hand because you can't go any further.

I am covered by the Blood of Jesus, He is my sanctuary and fortress, my border and boundary is laid out by my faith in Him, my destiny has been ordained by Him before the foundations of the Earth and before I was formed in my Mommy's womb.

I love You, Father, Son, and Holy Spirit. With you, I can do all the things that you have called me to do. No one is allowed to take me off track. Woe to the man or woman who tries to come in between me and my Lord. I need Him to walk with me today.

In Jesus's name, Amen and Amen.

Look Forward, Not Back

Don't grieve over things; look forward to the new things that are about to happen.

Even though there are some things from my past that I miss, like the mission trips to Honduras, I look forward into the new things that God is doing in my life. I glean from the past, which are the important things in my life. But now they are gone, I know that He is up to something new and fresh. He has a good plan and destiny for my life.

Protected by God

Read Psalms 23 and 91.

He is my protector, my provider, my provision, my all in all.

For myself, I am going through a time when Psalms are critical in my life. I have shared with a few of you what is going on in my life, and I know whether I have told you or not that all of you will continue to pray for me.

Even as I sit with my enemies and the main enemy tries to destroy my life, I know that He has the plan to keep me safe for He is good and knows everything and has brought me here to work through me. Standing and knowing He is God and will work everything out is sometimes easier said than done. Once I give it to Him, I need to stop trying to figure it out.

So reading and remembering the Psalms brings me to remember, for one, that He loves me and that He will take care of me when no man on earth can.

A Pastor Is Like a Parent

You know you have done your job right if other Ministries are launched from your teachings, like a parent. Our children are meant to grow up and become independent of us so that they can lead fulfilling lives. We need to do the same thing as Pastors. Don't continue to tell your flock to learn what God wants them to do, then try to keep them with you forever.

Nothing should be more satisfying than to be told when you get to Heaven, "Well done, my good and faithful servant," and getting to meet all the people who you helped along the way to fulfilling their calling in life, but above all, knowing that it was God all along and that you were the vessel He chose to use. He is so awesome!

Be blessed today and always.

Chasing Jesus

Amen, Amen, and Amen! We need to enjoy each season of our lives; some just seem to be better than others.

All I know is that I am running as fast after Jesus as I can, and when He sends the right one, I will know because he will be running just as fast alongside me.

I want to be the kind of person I would want to be with in a relationship. I want to be giving 100 percent to the relationship to come. It isn't fifty-fifty that makes a whole, it is one hundred-one hundred.

These are exciting times to be in His will for our lives. Touching a person at a time and knowing that we are all beautiful in His sight. Come together in agreement that we need to work together for His Glory and that He has a special purpose for each of our lives.

I guess that is what I like the most about ministering online is that I am seeing all of you blossom and bloom where He has planted you in the world. Encouraging and uplifting words are not only coming out of my team's mouths, but from all of you who visit this ministry online. I love letting my little light shine and seeing your lights too. Wow, lighting up the world with a spectrum of color; that shows how much love He can pour through us to touch our fellow man! Isn't that exciting?

Helping Others Find Jesus

We have so much work to do to help get our friends and family ready to meet Jesus with us. I want to be in Heaven and look around and see them all there with me. I don't want anyone who is not there to be able to say of me, "Why didn't you tell me?"

Seed, water, and harvest. I may not be able to provide all three for one person, but working together, we will see the fruits of our labors. I want to thank everyone who has taken part and contributed to my online ministry, and I encourage you to stand up for what you believe. This isn't the time to keep Jesus to ourselves but share Him with the world because He is coming back sooner than we think.

I want all of us to be in Heaven together. We may not meet in the world, but what a wonderful thing to recognize all of you in Heaven sitting and listening to the Father, Son, and Holy Spirit together.

Can you imagine? Now we need to get back to the work ahead of us and do all the things that we are destined to do for His glory and His Kingdom. We can do all things through Him, and remember, He works through us who believe in Him.

Words Are Power

Are you killing your own faith in what God does for you by your words?

Listen to Perry Stone's message. He talks about how we misuse our words to hurt and hold on to emotional wounds that have allowed things in our lives that we wish weren't there.

Words are power and can destroy you! Start speaking good things over yourself. We need to lift each other up!

A Prayer for Trials and Tribulations

Dear Father,

I come before YOU this morning with my petitions, not only for myself, but for my friends and family. Before I do that, I want to thank You for Your special gift of Jesus Christ, Your Son, and all that He did for me.

I come humbly before You in my pursuit to pray happiness and health and provisions, but most of all wisdom, not only for myself, but for my family and friends.

Father, in this day, we need more than enough. Not only for ourselves, but enough that we can help our fellow man, that when someone says, "I need your help," that we can reach into our pocket and help that person or we can provide a meal or whatever is needed.

I ask for direction in how and when I am supposed to supply that need. I ask that I am the one who can direct them to where they need to go to learn how to fish to last a lifetime and not the one that just hands them enough to just last them for the day. Please don't let me pass an opportunity to show the Love of Jesus. Let Him shine through me.

Father, I ask that if I have offended anyone that they forgive me and that our relationship is mended for Your glory. I ask that I am able to forgive anyone who has offended me intentionally or unintentionally and that relationships are mended for Your glory.

Father, I ask that You bring to the forefront of my memory people I need to pray for or call them, that I do it when they come to my mind and not wait, knowing that they are in need at the time, and that is why I am thinking of them.

Father, I ask for divine appointments, divine opportunities, and divine connections that bring transformation in not only my life, but those that I connect with for Your glory. Not that I can boast about for myself, but boast about You, and I can share with others on how good You are in my life. I ask that You cleanse anything out of me that is not of you. I ask for protection and Your guidance in all things, big and small. I ask that I give credit where credit is due; that too is You or through someone that You have used to bring about something good in my life. Ultimately, it all comes back to Your intervention in all that occurs in my life. I will remember Psalms 23 and 91 that have been provided for me to cover me and shield me in these days of trials and tribulations.

Father, I thank You for all of my family, and I ask that You bless them and keep them. I ask for my friends that You do the same. For the relationships that have come into my life that are truly like family to me, a special double anointing for they are the ones who truly under-

stand who I am and who I stand for. All in all, the people that you placed in my life were the divine appointments, the divine opportunities, and the divine connections. I ask for more people to come into my life that I can share Your love.

I thank You for the Pastors and Prophets, Apostles and the Evangelists, and teachers that have come into my life. They have fed me Your word, and I have gotten fat on their teaching to get me ready for the things that I need to do for You. I thank You that they have given me a step up into my destiny. Most of all, I just want to thank You for who You are!

In Jesus's name. Amen and Amen.

God's Bucket List

Do you have a "bucket list" of things you want to do for the Lord? What are some of the things in your bucket for Him?

—Paul Cobb

Well, Paul, my bucket list overflows! There is not time enough in a day it seems like, but then I look at all the time I wasted concerning myself with myself. Recently, I was looking at a CD I had made of the picture I took while in Honduras and realized that I would really like to see those people again. I still have the book in me that needs to be written about the Mission trips there.

I think of the books to be written, the songs to be sung, the artwork to be created. The list is endless. Then there is the What-If List…What if every day I asked Him, "Lord, what do You want me to do today? Where should I go? Who shall I see? What will I do to just please you?" It isn't about me, but it is about me, you see, when I know it was Him who lives in me and directs my path.

I recently heard a young Pastor ask this question: "Where is the wealthiest place on Earth? The answer is the graveyard." "Well, how can that be?" I asked myself. Then his answer was so clear. Because the books that were supposed to be written never got written, the songs that were supposed to be sung never got sung, the art that was supposed to be create never got done.

Okay, now how full is your bucket? I still haven't even begun to empty mine.

Serving Others Pays a Great Return

I am so excited! I had a wonderful Christmas where I could give to others, and guess what, it was a Christmas meal. I helped several other people serve the homeless in Fort Myers, Florida. It reminded me of the days I went with Team Jesus, and Bill and Charlene Cameron would have been cheering me on.

My friend came and picked me up Christmas Eve so we could get an early start in the morning. She was gracious to me and let me sleep until 8:00 a.m. instead of 6:00 a.m. She didn't know I got up several times because I didn't want to hold up anything.

We drove to Fort Myers, Florida, and this is how good God is. The very things we had talked about the night before and that morning were on a T. D. Jakes CD. I swear confirmation all over that CD. Powerful. Then we got there, and a crowd of people were there waiting. Oh man, you should have seen the spread—chicken and pork ribs so tender and juicy, mashed potatoes with garlic and butter, vegetables sautéed in butter and herbs, lasagna like from Italy itself, and then the desserts—I swear it was like we were being served like royalty.

It reminds me of the story when the big guys were invited to the wedding, and they were too busy to come, but the people that were meant to be there came. It was beautiful. The babies, the men, and the women—

smiles and laughter filled the air. I went around taking pictures of all these beautiful people who, for one day, could forget all of their problems and enjoy not only a good meal, but other people's company in conversation and laughter.

Yesterday, we celebrated our King's birth, but He didn't stay a baby, but He grew up to lay down His life to save us from destruction. He died for us and rose again and sits at the right hand of His Father, but yesterday as we served others, He walked amongst the people and blessed them in a special way.

I wouldn't have missed this for the world. I look forward to next year and doing it again. Oh wait, I don't think I will have to wait. Pastor Gasper Anastasi invited us to come back on New Year's Eve. He said we could help again.

Okay, when we do something like this, we sometimes think we are blessing others, but the truth is we are the ones getting the blessing. I feel all warm and comfy inside. I love You, Jesus, and You make my world rock with joy, and I feel loved so much by You when I can serve others as You have served me.

Renewed and Refreshed

I need a little Eagle power this morning! Come soar with me and see the goodness that the Lord has for you today. Be renewed and refreshed like the Eagle.

Soaring together to new heights in Him.

Ask for Help

Sometimes when I am disappointed in myself, I stop and remember who made me in His image, and then remember I can do all things with His help. Eagles and Eaglets, rise up and be all that you can be. He is with us!

Let God Drive, You Rest Awhile

Sometimes do you feel like life is a little overwhelming?

I do, and if I don't get the sleep I need during the night, I have to lay myself down to quiet my spirit so I can hear His spirit. Life is a journey, and if we let Him guide us, things that seem overwhelming to our human minds become as liquid gold when He intervenes.

So today if you feel a little overwhelmed, stop, take a deep breath, and let Him know you want Him to take control.

Finding Our Place

Sometimes, He makes us miserable when we are in the wrong place so that we can move into the place we belong.

This happened with my last job. It has happened to others. I want to hear His voice, so I don't have to go through tough times again. Sometimes we think it was the enemy, but God was walking with us all along. I don't know about you, but sometimes it seems I have gone through certain valleys more than once. Unfortunately, to me, that means I must not have learned what I was supposed to learn the first time.

Please, Father, give me clarity in every situation. Let me hear Your voice alone, no others that could cause me confusion. I have a direct line to You...through Your son Jesus Christ.

I am thankful I do not have to go through any person or thing to get to You. Leaving my past behind, I look forward to all the lovely things that You have in store for me. Use me to help others and, when needed, speak through me that they know it is You that I glorify and not myself.

I ask that all who read this hears Your voice, and when they have a problem after they give it to You, they let you do what you need to do and that they don't go pick it up again. We give You all the glory!

In Jesus's name, Yeshua! Amen and Amen.

Join Margene's online ministry through Facebook and get support you need from fellow Christians to grow in your daily walk with God!

If you are interested in contributing and learning from Margene Wiese-Baier's online ministry and growing in your daily walk with God with the support of other like-minded Christians, please join our groups on Facebook:

"I Must Be about My Father's Business" Reaching the Nations!

Fishers of Men Outreach

Sunwhisp's Christian Singles Corner

Sunwhisp's Christian Marriage Corner

Sunwhisp's Notes and Quotes, and Art to Inspire and Bring Glory to Jesus

Designs by Sunwhisp

Sunwhisp's Scammer Patrol

Angels in Flight II

Margene Wiese-Baier

Dedicated to my Mom and Dad...

Words are power and, when written down, last forever. I grew up watching my Mom write songs, poems, and novels. My heart broke when she went to Heaven before her time. Most of her works went unpublished, but she left a legacy of love for writing and a passion for art. I have found that these mingle together in perfect harmony.

From my first book Angels in Flight, I couldn't seem to say it better to honor my Mom. Even though she is not here on Earth, she is watching from Heaven, and I know she is happy knowing that her Legacy is being carried on not only by me, but my family, with Dad's support and encouragement and him telling me Mom would be so happy. I would like to also dedicate this book to my children and grandchildren who have brought me love and joy throughout this Journey we call Life! I hope throughout this book that people see above all that I put Abba Father, Jesus, and Holy Spirit at the Helm, and that HE leads me in everything I do! My Rock and Salvation, my very reason I strive to work in a Spirit of Excellence.

Extra Note!
I chose to leave this in the format that I used on Facebook, leaving the dates when written.

Contents

I Am Amazed by You!

I have to say I am Amazed by YOU! I was thinking about my life and the Amazing things that YOU have done for me. How I almost died instantly in March of 2009, and I asked YOU if YOU were ready to take me Home and then said to YOU, but if YOU still had work for me to do, I am willing to stay. Some days I wished YOU would have just taken me Home because it was so hard. YOU had to be my Husband, My Provider and Provision, because sometimes I had no clue where the money was going to come from. People would ask me where I got the money. In some cases, I could not even tell them, but GOD...

And you know what? It is really no one's business how GOD provides the money, but it is important to give HIM the Glory for moving others to help when you are trying to serve HIM. Okay, I am not a well-known Pastor or Evangelist or even a well-known Prophet, but I know I was hearing from HIM every step of the way. I was not able to work because of being hurt that day, but people would have had me work at McDonalds. I knew that I might be pleasing people, but not HIM. HE has given me talents and gifts that were lying dormant that HE was just waiting for me to use.

I was using my gift of writing and photography for Facebook and even promoting others. But I hadn't used them for me. I had to learn who I was in HIM in order to graduate in my calling and gifting. I wanted to fly like an Eagle, but at best, I felt like I was plucked and just ready for a Chicken coop. Oh my, how I wanted to fly. I remember the day I asked the question about still having work to do, but I let what others said to stop me. The enemy would seem to grab me at my jugular vein and try to stop me from speaking up for myself. Telling me that I needed to be more like so and so if I wanted work with them. Hey, you know GOD made me this way for a reason. And I am now knowing if I wanted a friend, I would really like me.

Of course, as a KING'S KID, I can say that. Because HE loves me. I now know everyone doesn't have to love me, and they don't even have to like me. And I am finally okay with that. As long as I know I am treating people as I would like to be treated. I am still working on my healing, and I am willing to apologize if I hurt someone. Forgiveness is a wonderful freeing feeling. The thing is to really mean it.

Just think if GOD can forgive me and start fresh with me daily. I think I can too. Anyway, it is something I am working on. OK, that is one thing you will find with me: I am honest. Sorry, men, I don't put up with much. When I love you, I really love you. And hey, if you say it to me, you better mean it. And you know what Words without action is WORTHLESS. WORDS ARE POWER. I HAVE HAD REJECTION ENOUGH TO FILL A LIFETIME. BUT you KNOW WHAT? IT WAS FOR MY PROTECTION. Not just from Men but Women too.

So if you like me, you like me. If not, I am not going to be offended any longer. Actually, I am growing through that. Because I don't have time to play any games with people. Those games are just the enemy's way to distract me for what I am supposed to do for HIM. Love is the answer, and HIS Promises HE will keep, so if we work together for HIS Glory, we will accomplish a lot more. So let's learn to fly together like the Eagles. I LOVE YOU, Lord Jesus Christ. My Abba Father, trusting YOU is worth everything. And Holy Spirit, Thank YOU for being the Wind beneath my wings. Soaring together, we shall help Unite not only America but the World. Love all of you, Eagles and Eaglets. Let's Soar Higher and Higher.

Childlike Faith

Do you have Childlike faith? I pray that you remember the first day that you fell in love with JESUS. It should be the most Wonderful Memory that you have. I don't remember the exact date, but I do know who first told me about HIM. That was my Mother.

My Mom was wonderful and is now in Heaven since 1985. It is a wonderful Gift that you can give to your Children. You may not be perfect and you may make a lot of mistakes on the way, but if you can hold on to the LOVE of JESUS, you will be OK. And Well, Give the Gift of JESUS today, and remember your Childlike Faith. All is Well! In the Name of JESUS. Amen and Amen. Shalom! A good thing. Whoop-Whoop. ♥ ♥

Remembering and Being Thankful for Mothers and Fathers
© 2009

At some point last night, it was like I heard within me that I need to be thankful for something that happened a long time ago. I even had pondered on it during the night, but apparently still asleep, so I didn't write it down. And then it was gone. I was so disappointed because it seemed God was trying to tell me something important. Oh, God, bring it back to my remembrance I began to say over and over again. And all that I was getting is to be thankful to Mother and Father for their part in bringing me into existence.

And now I ponder some more about the importance of who our parents are in who we become in life. My Mom was a Writer-Author and wrote poems, songs, novels, and on and on; she was also an Artist. She also was kindhearted and generous to a fault and never said an unkind word against anyone, and if she did, she always brought it back around to the positive in the good of the person. Somehow, it got conveyed to me that even if someone says something derogatory about someone that I should not judge the person talked about, because that is the perception of the speaker, and my perception might be completely different if I met that person. Okay, back to being thankful for my Mom and Dad. My Mom brought me up to think about others before myself. Sometimes that is a good thing and sometimes not so good. But if I can get my eyes off my own problems and focus on helping someone else, I feel better about the things I am going through. My Mom was easy to talk to and kept it to herself what a person told her. I think that is why if a person tells me something one day and asks me if I remember, it has already been forgotten, and that is how I know I won't pass someone else's business to someone else. My Mom is now in Heaven, and I truly miss her but know I will see her again someday. Being close to Christmas time, it is harder because that was my Mom's favorite time of year.

Then there is my Dad. I always thought I was Dad's favorite. Now my brothers and sister would probably debate me on this point and possibly win. But isn't it true every little girl wants to be their Daddy's favorite? My Dad and I have a special bond that not all people have with their Dad's, and that saddens me. When I was growing up, I wanted to learn to cook and my Mom would let me try things on my own, and my Dad would actually eat them. Sorry, Dad, I am just glad you didn't go into the Hospital for some of them concoctions. Well, I did learn to cook. My Dad was a hard worker and provided very well for us. Sometimes, I wish that he didn't have to work so hard and could have spent more time with us. But the biggest thing I remember is that he took us on Adventures to see my Grandmother and her husband Doc and my Uncle John and trips to see my Uncle and Aunt and my ten cousins. My Dad was not big on plans, but he was adventurous and spontaneous, and I think that is where I get it. I am not saying the important things aren't planned out, but the fun things need to just happen for me, and I think I got that from my Dad. I like it, I like it a lot.

I think I am thinking and pondering about all of this because here it is another Christmas, and this year, I am still on my own. My family is far away, and even though I want to be with them, it isn't going to happen. But I have the good Memories of Christmas Past when I was with them. My own children are grown now with their own little families that even though I am not with them physically, I am with them in Spirit during this Christmas Holiday.

As far as Mothers go, I think of Jesus's mother Mary. How she said yes to be His Mom. A big job for sure. Even though I don't worship or pray to her, I am still thankful to her for saying yes and being obedient for such a big responsibility. Being a Mother is one of the hardest jobs I know of.

Then Joseph saying yes and not wimping out in being Jesus's Dad, that was huge. Not just any man would have said yes to such a big job. God knew whom He could trust with such an endeavor.

Both Mary and Joseph were the Mother and Father to our best gift this and every Christmas which is Jesus Christ. Our own parents did their part by saying yes to bringing us into the World though not a perfect World, but a place where each one of us have our part in making it a better place to live. We don't have as big of job as Jesus did, but we have our part in telling and teaching others in what He did for them.

I think Christmas should be celebrated every day. Not the part of giving gifts or even the part about Jesus just being born, but the part that He still exists today, and Christmas is just a reminder of where His life began on earth.

JUST A THOUGHT. OR IS IT?

I HOPE THIS BLESSED YOU AS MUCH AS IT HAS BLESSED ME IN WRITING IT. REMEMBER, I LOVE YOU WITH THE LOVE OF JESUS.

HUGS, MARGENE

I Believe!

John 3:16-17 For God so loved the World that He sent His only Begotten Son that whosoever believes in Him will not perish but have everlasting Life. For God did not send His Son into the world to condemn the world, but that the world through Him might be saved."

I am a Supernatural being having a Human experience. To just be a Human would be boring.

I believe there is a God that is here to help us, and I believe there is an enemy that is here to torment us.

I believe there is a Heaven and a Hell. They are both very real.

I believe that God sent His Son Jesus to die and be raised from the dead and to go back to Heaven to sit at His right side, so I can go to Heaven myself one day.

I believe He knew me before the very foundation of the World and that He mapped out a Plan and a Purpose for my Life. As it is said in Jeremiah 29:11: "For I know the plans I have for you," declares the Lord, "plans to prosper you and not to harm you, plans to give you hope and a future."

I do not hold lightly the things the LORD has given me. To HIM, I give all of the Glory! People will come and go in my life, but HE will walk beside me for all Eternity. HE is a JUST GOD and looks into the Heart of every believer. I am excited to see all that HE has revealed to me. As I write I am seeing New revelations of where I have been and where HE is bringing me too. HE has brought me out to bring me IN. I LOVE HIM more today than yesterday. A BELIEVER in JESUS.

Ask HIM how HE sees you and I know HE will call you Son or Daughter.

Victory in Jesus.

Love and Abundant Blessings, Margene/Sunwhisp ♥

Humbled

I am Humbled and so blessed by many of you that have continued to show me Love and respect. God has shown me much about myself. If you ask, HE shows you who we really are. HE has brought many things back to my Memory about my life. The good and the bad. The people that I have loved more than they loved me. The people that didn't love themselves enough to know how much God loved them. HE has shown me the Prophesies that have yet to be fulfilled. HE has brought back the words that HE gave me that no one else had been told. Even the things that HE gave others, but they would not give me because they just could not see me as what God was showing them. I am finding the best Prophesies is from people you don't know me. Like Jesus's family and people in his own hometown did not accept who HE was. I want to encourage everyone that has a word from the Lord. Even though it has not come to pass yet. I say YET, because GOD is a Promise Keeper. Keep believing. It is an exciting day we live in. I believe Abba Father is speaking. Quiet yourself and Listen. HE is waiting to speak to you. Love is the Answer. Speak it loudly. Many need to hear you. Most of all for you to demonstrate it. Hugs, Margene.

Indecision/Decision

It's confusing when you're trying to make a decision that is going to change your life forever. When you finally make that decision and stick with it, it is like having the feeling of complete triumph—that a weight like a two-ton elephant has been lifted off your shoulders. The sticking with it is the hard part. Especially when you have friends and family that don't want you to change.

When I decided to get a divorce, so much life got in the way it took years to finally go through with the process. Was it life or fear? Being afraid of losing my children. Wow, what a revelation. I had forced that one back into the storage banks of my mind. You know the part where you put things you really don't want to deal with because to deal with them would be far too painful. My kids were my life. Afraid that I would be making a huge mistake because he really was a pretty good guy, wasn't he?

Just because my self-esteem was nonexistent and just because I felt no one else would love and accept me the way I was—like he did.

He needed me. I was there to help him, save him. Save him from what? Being an alcoholic, from self-destructing? Combusting and going completely mad? Going through Milestones Alcohol Treatment Center with him was pure Hell for me. Having to listen to how bad he felt for all his other girlfriends in how he had treated them. What about me? Wasn't I the one who was his wife and the mother of his children? For God's sake! What about me? Thank God! He finally sought the help of the VA (Veterans) to help him get over the hurdle of being in Vietnam. I did not want to even try to fathom the horror of being in a war that no one wanted to support, let alone come to terms with, and acknowledge that it really happened, but like the alcohol treatment, I stuck with him through all the pain of flashbacks and nightmares. So sad! He would be whimpering like a sad puppy when he was having a nightmare. Waking him, assuring him that it was only a bad dream and that no one was chasing him. I didn't want to hear what the dream was about because I didn't want to relive his horror in my own dreams

What I found is no one can save you; you have to save yourself. Once I found that truth, the decision to get a divorce was easy. Besides, I needed to save myself, and I wouldn't be able to do that in the confines of and unhealthy, unloving marriage.

Inside ourselves, we have an image, and ideal of what a happy marriage should look like, and my marriage didn't even come close to my internal perception of what that would be.

The worst thing about being in a bad relationship is that you can't give your children a good example of what a good loving healthy relationship should look and feel like.

I guess that is my biggest regret about not making the decision sooner is that I could have possibly gotten into a healthy relationship. It seemed every time I tried to get out of the marriage before; my children would talk me into staying. They would do this even though they were the ones that would tell me to divorce Dad because he's so mean to you. Wow! What the human heart does to contradict itself to stay in the familiar.

Love has always been important to me, and I always wondered why I couldn't love this man, but how easy it was to love the children we created together.

I yearned to be with my soul mate and came to the tearful conclusion that this man wasn't him. Not only was I sad for myself at this revelation, but I was sad for him because I knew he deserved to be with someone that loved and cherished him, and I knew I could no longer try to be that person, and I knew I deserved the same for myself.

It's amazing how the minutes, hours, and oh yes, the years just pass in a blink of an eye. A speck of time in the scheme of things.

Here I was at my wedding not knowing if I was doing the right thing. Even though I had a gut-wrenching feeling that I should not be going through with it, but then I said to myself, "If it happens, it must be meant to be." A decision not to make a decision is the worst decision of all because the decision usually turns out to be the wrong one.

That feeling long ago while standing in front of the minister when God was telling me I shouldn't marry this man. Maybe He was really telling me that this is just a small part of your life because if I wouldn't have gone through with the marriage, I wouldn't have had two beautiful daughters and a beautiful grandson that took twenty-one years to come into existence. What could be more gratifying than bringing life to children that could possibly make all your wrong decisions right— just by being.

So why did God give us a brain anyway just to let life happen to us or for us to make our lives the best we can.

Now I know it is our duty as human beings to use or intelligence God gave us to make good decisions.

If we really listen, He will even help us. It may be that gut-wrenching feeling, a friendly word whispered in our ear, a gentle tug at a corner of our heart, or that nagging little thought that runs helter-skelter through the recesses of our minds.

Life is a learning experience. I hope I learned what I needed to learn and now I have a second chance.

Not a chance to go back and change the past, but the chance to change the future into something that I can be proud of. Regrets are futile and not worth my energy. I am ready to fulfill my destiny; I hope I will do something that will leave a loving imprint on all humanity. Or at least I know that from now on my decisions will be the right decisions, so I can continue my saga of life in dignity.

One Day You Found Me

One day you found me
All Crumpled and Ashamed
Like a Crumpled Piece of Paper in the Rain
My Story was written
And I had nothing to gain
I felt like a sad little Urchin
And I felt a lot of pain

Then you found me
And my life has never been the same
You gave me the Will to live again
My story was rewritten
Then I had everything to gain

How can I repay you?
Only You can know
Because You loved me
When I had nothing to Show
You took my crumpled little life
And took out the Strife
You made it plain
That I had everything to gain

Now I walk in Victory
And a Love renewed
I give everything
I have to give to YOU
For I gave myself
That is all that You asked
But YOU gave me more
When You died upon the Cross
My Sins have been forgiven
And all that I know
I will live with YOU forever
The Lover of my Soul

I now have the Victory
And know YOU will never go
You carried me when
I did not know what to do

So

I worship You
I Praise Your Name
'Cause my life will never be the same
Hallelujah
Hallelujah
Hallelujah
You are so Worthy to be Praised

Dream Squelcher or Dream Maker

"Are you a DREAM Squelcher or A DREAM MAKER!" You have met people that squash your dreams. As soon as you start talking about your dream, they tell you that they just can't see you that way. We all know people like that because they don't want you to move forward. It is like the Crabs in a pot. Every time a crab tried to crawl out of the pot of boiling water, two or three crabs got together and pulled that crab back down in the pot because if they were going to die, they all were going to die. Friends like that may not want you to die, but they sure want your dreams to die. Which I call the DREAM SQUELCHERS!

Then there are people that are the ones that sees what God sees in you. They are the ones that will encourage you to Dream as large as you can. They are the ones that will allow the Holy Spirit to Prophesy through them. Sometimes even surprising themselves with what comes out of their mouths. These people even though they might not see everything that God shows you. They will not belittle you, realizing that they know how it feels when someone does that to them. They will stand by you if someone tries to make you feel defeated.

The thing is we should always be willing to try and never give up on ourselves and to encourage others to fulfill their dreams too.

So don't be a dream squelcher, but a DREAM MAKER!

Margene Wiese-Baier

Well, it is Saturday morning! And I have had my coffee. The first one always tastes the best too me. The freshness I guess...

This morning, I am going to try to speak those things that are not as if they were...

The one thing I know is I am truly thankful for all the Blessings that my FATHER has given me.

And to have a good earthly Father and a family that loves me is important too.

To have a family that isn't blood related but by JESUS shows me that they love me is a plus...

But knowing when I pray, I have to pray as if whatever it is the answer is already here or being manifested because I need to pray, knowing that I am praying the things that HE already approves of...

Wanting health for others, wanting love for others, wanting financial breakthroughs for other, and knowing HE wants those same things for me, but above all, praying for WISDOM in all things...

Remembering Dreams do come true 'cause I am witnessing them all around me. I will continue that my KING is the Dream Maker and LOVES me like no other. HE is the one who sends in the right people for everything in my life and yours. Continue to BELIEVE and you shall RECEIVE all that HE has for you.

LOVE KNOWS no BOUNDARIES!

The only Boundaries you need to set are the ones for the enemy. JESUS came to give life to the full. That means to me, HE wants us to be HAPPY!

HE has the plan for your life, and HE knew you before the Foundations of the World and before you were formed in your Mother's Womb.

Keep up the good works for HIS GLORY!

Margene/Sunwhisp ♥ ♥

When You Pray. Believe!

When you pray, Believe and have Faith that God will answer you. Pray fervently and effectual. My prayer partner and I were discussing this. Do you realize that God looks forward to us coming to HIM in prayer? Prayer is a conversation we have with our BESTEST of FRIENDS, our FATHER in HEAVEN. We were taught through the Prayer that JESUS taught us to start out with FATHER and then we learned to end in JESUS'S NAME. Don't stop praying for something until it comes to pass. If you know that it is something that you know is in GOD'S WILL. Remember that when there are other people involved that you cannot, and HE will not go against their wills. Don't pray that you will get someone Else's husband or wife; that is Witchcraft. Remember when others are involved, the answer may take time because God has to work behind the scenes with several people. God will not give you things that will hurt you. I always prayed when I was involved with a man that they could not even come and meet me if they weren't being sent by HIM. You know how many men that God Closed the door. LOL. I even told some of them that God would close the door if they weren't from HIM...they did not believe me, but guess what? God did not allow them to come. I even prayed no more counterfeits, and I did not meet anyone for years, and I stayed off the internet because I did not want to meet on the Internet, and as soon as I got on, the enemy tried again. But GOD... Honor God today and go to HIM; don't do all the talking. HE has something HE wants to tell you.

Love, Margene http://biblehub.com/james/5-16.htm

Photo by: Margene Wiese-Baier. God's Master Art.

Margene Wiese-Baier http://biblehub.com/james/5-16.htm

James 5:16 "Therefore confess your sins to each other and pray for each other so that you may be."

Confess your faults one to another and pray one for another that you may be healed. The effectual fervent prayer of a righteous man avails much.

BIBLEHUB.COM

Everything Has a Time and a SEASON

Everything has a time and a SEASON. Open Doors...Closed Doors... New Beginnings...Time to put things away...Time to reflect. So today, Check in with the LORD and see what SEASON you are in. Congratulations to all that have gotten Married in the last Couple of days, for all of those in New Relationships, for all of those that have a new life that has come into their lives, for all the Children that have new Dads and Moms, Adopting into a loving family, Bringing Husbands and Wives back together. There are so many things to give God all of the Glory as we pray for each other IN JESUS'S NAME. Hallelujah!

One Day You Walked into My Life!

One day you walked into my Life.
And then I thought you walked away.
But it was just the Break I needed.
And it succeeded to show me things that I needed to see.
They say that Absence makes the heart fonder.
And that is exactly what it did.
I needed God to heal some things in me.
And in doing that, HE healed some things in you too.
HE helped us both to mature and to see the things we needed to see.
Sometimes, the little boy and girl inside of us comes out and brought all the pain from the past, but the time we spent away from each other allowed them to grow up.

Not saying they will never appear again, but if they do, we can let them know that they have someone that loves us enough to understand and hold us till the insecurity passes.

We got Stronger in the Absence, so we can come back together. For Love never Fails, and God is leading the Way. Being Thankful that God brought us back full Circle. Like the Wedding Ring of Never-ending Love. Thank you for walking back into my life.

Dedication, a Wonderful Word

Wow, Dedication, what a wonderful word, and it holds so much meaning. God has been showing me different people to be Dedicated too. Showing me that HE has a PURPOSE and a PLAN for their lives, and I am to be a part of that to help Propel them forward. Showing me what I made happen for them. God will bring someone that will do the same for me. There are Gifts and Talents that have gone unnoticed. Until. Until. Until now. By being Dedicated to others. Ya neva know what God will do. They may be the next Person that will impact the World. Let HIM show you who to be Dedicated to and for those that you should release. Just a thought or is it? Margene/Sunwhisp ♥

Sometimes it is that a person just needs a hand up, not a handout, and as they rise to the top, they will remember that you helped them and reach back to give you a hand to pull you forward too. Sometimes, it isn't about the money that you could charge to get the job done, but your wiliness to help them because you see their potential. Seeing things that could be is the key you need to make things happen. Seeing those things that are not as if they were. Just a thought or is it? Margene/Sunwhisp ♥
PS: It only takes one person to see you the way God sees you to help you get to your Destination. 2012

Margene Wiese-Baier

For truly, as we look at the definition of FAITH, and we learn it is the substance of things hoped for and the evidence of things not yet visible or felt in the natural; how else can we get there and see those things that are not as though they are except by way of a sanctified imagination?

As Jesus said: "All things are possible if ONLY you can believe!"

It Is a Relationship. Not a Religion.

It is funny. Today I was asked, "How long have you been born again?" And I answered that I have always loved Jesus. She said, "No, how long have you been Born Again?" Feeling put on the spot, I answered her, almost feeling intimidated on further thinking about it. When I accepted Jesus as a child, I accepted the Holy Spirit and God. I do remember as a teenager going up front of the Church several time because the way they put it. It made me feel I needed to, so again I will say, I have loved Jesus from a young age but have grown in all ways with HIM. I am no longer that little Lutheran Girl, but bravely go to the Front of the Church and dance with my King. Yes, I speak in tongues, but I spoke to HIM in ways that I knew not of, ways before I knew that is what I was doing. So sometimes I wonder if as Christians, we act Holier than thou and make people feel as I did. It isn't about Religion, but about Relationship, and if asked about my Relationship, I could say I have had a Relationship with my King since a very small girl, but have grown in Wisdom and LOVE for HIM. We will draw them by LOVE, not by intimidation or judgment. Just a thought or is it? Margene/Sunwhisp ♥ She was asking me if I felt that I was backslidden. Just because a person is having a bad time does not mean they are backslidden. It could be that the enemy has been messing with them because he knows their potential.

There is such an Excitement that has been rising up in me. I have been a witness to many of my friends in seeing what God is doing in their lives. I am thankful for Answered prayers, giving me even more hope into what is about to come. God is showing me What I make happen for others, HE will make happen for me. Get Ready. Get Ready. Get Ready. Sow into other's lives. I am not just talking money; your time is more valuable. When you tell someone you are going to pray for them, do it. If you can pray with them right then and there. My problem is that if I leave them without praying, when I get home, I get busy with something else and I have forgotten all about my promise. And when I promise something, I mean it and then feel bad or even to the point of feeling guilty if I didn't do it. So today I pray for each of you to have a Divine appointment that gives you a Chance to Pray for someone, a chance to lead them to Jesus, which means a chance to pray for them. Give them a hug. Maybe they need to feel a human's touch, and when you give them a hug, pray that it is God's arms wrapped around them. As I was talking to my friend/prayer partner and she said we need to talk to men that come into our lives tenderly. I am thinking we need to talk to everyone tenderly because we do not always know what a person is going through your tenderness may just be what they need, and it may be what draws them to want what you have and that is Jesus. Come together for ME. Hallelujah! Let us be and go to the Extreme Love for we are Spiritual Beings having Human experiences. Let us be the ones helping others to have a happier more joyous experience here on Earth. Praying all of this in LOVE for GOD is LOVE. Hugging all of you tightly, Margene

Even pigs were purified when Jesus went to the cross for our sins. Everything unclean was made clean. Come on now. Jesus changed the

World when HE went to the Cross. Some people would like to continue to remind you of who you used to be, not letting you become who HE destined you to be. But you need to remind yourself of whom you belong. A KING'S Kid! A Prince or a Princess. Unique! Release the Negative and invite the Positive. Surround yourself with people that want the best for you. Is it Pruning time again? Those crabs that keep trying to pull you back down into to Pot, they need to just let you go. If they are satisfied to just cook and not move forward, you will just have to let them. You have things to do and places to go. Just a thought or is it. Love in Jesus.

I recently read a note from a person that people were unfriending her, and she could not understand why. It could be Facebook, or it could be God doing some pruning so you can grow. I feel it is important that you know not to be upset when people decide to leave our lives especially people we have never met. God is trying to move you forward, and some people are stopping you from what HE has for you. HE will keep people from meeting you personally because they are not part of your Destiny. I know we get so attached to people because we talk to them almost every day, but instead of filling us up, they are draining us. How often do you tell your Pastor that HE is making a difference in your Life?

You know they need encouragement too. They work hard to bring the Word of God to you. To speak into your life. How about this week you send your Pastor a word of Encouragement, a word of how much you appreciate them? A love gift! Okay, I am not saying it has to be Money, so don't get all thinking it is about Money. But hey, who does everything belong to anyway? GOD! But what if you gave your Pastor something that was Eternal? Pray about it. I believe Abba Father is saying the Ones that HE has given to you to be your encouragement need to hear from you to know that they are doing something that helps keep you on the right track. Knowing Jesus is the Way, the Truth, and the Life. And HE is the Light of the World. Just a Thought or is it? Love in Jesus, Margene Wiese-Baier 2017.

So lift up your Head and see that Abba Father is a Good God to protect us. Do not regret helping them for a Season, but their season in your life is over. HE is about to send in the ones that HE wants to help Propel you forward. A calling and a Destiny that not everyone can enter with you. Only a chosen few. Get Ready. Get Ready. Get Ready. It is going to be GOOD. Love in Jesus, Margene Wiese-Baier 2017

Preparation for Fruit!

Like this tree, we sometimes feel naked and bare and open to be seen to the very insides of us. The winter season in our lives when we feel like we really have nothing to give. But like this tree, we notice that little buds of life that are usually reserved for Spring are coming forth. But we know to hold on because we know it is not time yet because the harshness of the chill of Winter will cause the buds to not come forth in the promises because the warmth of the sun will not bring the Fruition of the fruit until the season is right. Even though we may not look ready, God is doing some work inside of us in preparing us for what HE has for us. Like this tree, it may look dead, but what is going on inside those branches God has been preparing it for the life. This will be evident when the leaves begin to come out and the fruit begins to grow. People can't fully enjoy that fruit until it is ripe. When it is ripe, it is sweet to the taste and more palatable. Don't regret or despise the times that you are being prepared, just keep moving forward in knowing that your FRUIT WILL BE SWEET AND PALATABLE. Your Journey may seem as bare as this tree, but if you look deep inside of you, you will see the growth and that GOD has great plans for you. You don't need to be like anyone else, and you have to know that GOD created you the way you are because HE DOESN'T NEED EVERYONE TO BE THE SAME, BUT HE LOVES VARIETY. JUST LOOK AT ALL OF THE ANIMALS, LOOK AT ALL THE PLANTS, LOOK AT THE STARS IN THE SKY. IF YOU LOOK CLOSELY, NONE ARE EXACTLY THE SAME. LEARN TO LOVE WHO YOU ARE. HE DOES. IT DOES NOT MATTER IF YOU FEEL THAT OTHERS DON'T UNDERSTAND YOU. HE DOES! HE is waiting to talk to you! Seek HIM and see what HE has to say to you, and above all,

DO NOT GIVE UP! HE HAS THE PLAN FOR YOUR LIFE, AND IT IS GOOD! JEREMIAH 29:11 Love, Margene Wiese-Baier

I Follow Jesus

I follow Jesus. I have many Pastors that I love, but I have found I cannot put any of them on a pedestal 'cause they are men and women (human), and if they fall off that pedestal, I am going to be disappointed. Recently, Kenneth Copeland told a news person that was asking him questions about why he needed. I think it was about his cars. Well, maybe it was about his jets or airplanes, why he needed so many. He told her it was none of her business. Well, it is the people's business that sow into that ministry. If he is using their money to purchase them. He can say none of their business if he is using his own money. Look at Jesse Duplantis Ministries, he once said that he doesn't need our money for the things he wants 'cause he makes his own. Check these things out, 'cause I am going by what I remember. I think no matter what the color, one thing is the same. We cannot put anyone higher than Jesus because that is making them an idol. God is not a man that He would lie, but you can see many men and women of God lying. And when they get caught having to beg us for forgiveness. Men and Women that represent God in the Pulpit or even on Social Media are held to a Higher accountability. The difference is if you have a Church building, people seem to think that you are worth sowing into. And sometimes that is a hard pill for us that are giving our all to do God's work the best we know how and even go where HE calls us to go to the Nations. We know that God supplies, but God uses people. So if I don't have the money, I just don't go. 'Cause I am not going to beg anyone for the money. Sorry, if I am being too real here. But we do need a little more balance in our giving. Margene

Don't Let Anyone Have Power over You!

Don't let anyone have power over you! Every time they come to your mind and you start to have negative thoughts about them because they hurt you, you just allowed the enemy to use that person to bring you down. Lift yourself up and say no to the devil and say I forgave that person and they are out of my life, and I am not going to allow you or them to hurt me anymore. I am no longer that person they hurt.

I am STRONG, CONFIDENT and I am the KING'S KID, and I don't have time to waste with this nonsense 'cause I have work to do for my KING. Yup! And that is that. Take that, you itty bitty devil. I got my Mind back and my Heart and I am Spiritually where I need to be. Moving Forward, not looking back. Let's go. Margene

(I discovered I was not the first one to use itty-bitty devil.)

Are you his TROPHY Wife or girlfriend? I remember a friend that was married to a very unattractive Pastor. She really loved him, but he just wanted someone that would make him look good. Their MARRIAGE soon dissolved because behind closed doors, he was mean to her. The TRUTH shall set you FREE!

The FATHER sees a Person's HEART! People who have a Beautiful HEART, the beauty will come to the surface. If the person has an ugly deceitful HEART, it will soon be evident to those around them.

Abba Father,

I am praying that you brighten my mind and cover it in your protection, that the enemy cannot send in anyone that will distract me from what YOU have me to do. To stay on the right course. Not to be fooled into thinking that they are for me because YOU have given me the gift of discernment. Focusing on YOU. I know that I can see what YOU want me to see. Do what YOU want me to do. I pray no more Counterfeits can cross my Path. I pray that anyone that I need in my life stays and the ones that are out to harm me leave. In Jesus's Name! I am Under YOUR Mighty Wings and am covered with Jesus's blood. Mighty is HE. In Jesus's Mighty Name. Love, Margene ♥

I Am Thankful for Answered Prayers...

There is such an Excitement that has been rising up in me. I have been a witness to many of my friends in seeing what God is doing in their lives. I am thankful for Answered prayers, giving me even more hope into what is about to come. God is showing me What I make happen for others, HE will make happen for me. Get Ready. Get Ready. Get Ready. Sow into others' lives. I am not just talking money, your time is more valuable. When you tell someone you are going to pray for them. Do it! If you can pray with them right then and there. My problem is that if I leave them without praying. When I get home, I get busy with something else and I have forgotten all about my promise. And when I promise something, I mean it and then feel bad or even to the point of feeling guilty if I didn't do it. So today I pray for each of you to have a Divine appointment that gives you a Chance to Pray for someone, a chance to lead them to Jesus. Which means a chance to pray for them. Give them a hug. Maybe they need to feel a human's touch, and when you give them a hug, pray that it is God's arms wrapped around them. As I was talking to my friend/prayer partner and she said we need to talk to men that come into our lives tenderly. I am thinking we need to talk to everyone tenderly because we do not always know what a person is going through; your tenderness may just be what they need, and it may be what draws them to want what you have and that is Jesus. Come together for ME. Hallelujah! Let us be and go to the Extreme Love Beings for we are Spiritual Beings having Human experiences. Let us be *the ones helping others to have a happier more joyous experience here on Earth. Praying all of this in LOVE for GOD is LOVE. Hugging all of you tightly, Margene.*

Photo by Margene Wiese-Baier

God's Blueprints

I was going to post this with the abortion post, but it is a more positive note and deserves a place of its own.

It always amazes me how our human body is so wonderfully made. How skillfully Our Father had to be in creating us. Can you imagine what the Blueprints looked like? Did HE have to make notes? Did HE have to think about it. HE JUST SPOKE and BREATHED into the first man. Transformed the dust from the Ground and voila. A Human was formed. Created, then Woman was created from the man's Rib. No wonder it is said we become one when we get married. OH LORD, HOW I LOVE YOU. In Jesus's Name. Margene/Sunwhisp 🩷 ♥ © 2012

It's God's Rainbow

One thing that I have been thinking about. That has been on my mind is that the Rainbow should not represent the Gay population, but the many colors of People that represent our World—God's Creation. I wrote a song about the Love that we should have for each other. And the truth is that if we are cut, we all bleed red.

This Christmas, I would like everyone to forget that they dislike someone because of their color, but to embrace them and know beyond knowing that God is not going to put us in different sections.

Do you ever imagine what Heaven will be like? I do! OH my, the person that may have lived in a Shack on earth may have a bigger Mansion than the one that had a Mansion on earth.

How can you make this a better World? It may be just a smile, a hug, a sandwich, a cup of water. What if you started today just speaking a kind word to that person that you have been avoiding just because they don't look like you? Actually! I have to admit that there are some women of color that are more beautiful to me. For you see, when God made us, HE wanted us all to be Unique and beautiful. But HE didn't take one mold but created many. And HE brought out HIS Paint Pallet and said, "I painted a white baby a little while ago. Let me paint this child a soft Chocolate color, with dark brown eyes Or maybe even blue, because the Daddy has blue eyes because he fell in love with a dark-eyed beauty with the skin color of ebony."

I love the way GOD interacts in our lives to bring people together. We need to get over that we need to Marry within our own race or color. It amazes me when reading the Bible that HE brought us together through these things that some put their nose up at. So the next time you see a Japanese person with a sugar-white person, rejoice, the next you see an Indian person with a white person. Know this: God brought them together for a reason. And that reason is HE had a Divine Purpose and a Plan for them to impact the World. HE is still going to bring the same races together. And that amazes me too that they may not have met in their own Country, but after coming to America, HE brings them together.

So as I said, the Rainbow should represent the PEOPLE that Abba Father made to inhabit the World. Appreciate who HE made you to be. And seek HIM to see what HE would want you to be. For it is Good. Remember the enemy is out to Kill, Steal, and Destroy. You can't allow the itty bitty devil to mess with you or you can allow Our Father to bring you into fulfill what HIS plan is for you.

I chose to LOVE all colors of the Rainbow. The colors of the People of the World.

And by the way we need to stop Stereotyping people for what a few do. In every nationality, there are good people and bad. Let us see people how Jesus sees them.

Love, Margene Wiese-Baier Christmas Eve

Looking forward to a great New Year, but want to go out with a Bang in this year! A Love bang! Shalom! Peace, be Still!

What good is reading the Bible Word if you don't believe the word? I think that is what Pastor Mark Pothier just wrote. Even though I thought of this several times, I will not take the credit for the first one who thought it or wrote it. But in saying that how is it that we can read the Bible all of the time yet have no clue on what it really means. Today when you read the Bible, ask the Holy Spirit to enlighten you on what the writers are trying to tell us. Especially when Jesus is speaking. God gave us a brain for a reason. He gave us a Heart to feel. I have been told to pray without emotion. Really, even at the time, I was told that I could no way not feel when I prayed. To not feel emotion would not feel HIS presence. I know my GOD feels, I know that HE thinks. I know that HE gave me these things because HE has them HIMSELF.

Listen to HIM. Feel HIS Presence. Sense HIS direction. Learn to discern. Understand HIS word with the help of the HOLY SPIRIT. Anointing is the blessing of all things that HE wants to give us. Speaking through us. Hallelujah!

Giving HIM all of the Glory. Remember, HE is wanting the best for us. Love, Margene

Opening Doors!

God is opening the Doors for many! Are you going to walk through them, or let your past keep you from what God has Destined you for? Some of you are the ones that will help give to others that nudge or push to help them get to where they need to be. By doing that, you are not only helping them, but you will see God's Manifestations in your own life. What you make happen for others, God will make happen for you. Watch, See, and Expect to be all that you can be. God is waiting to talk to you. Don't believe me. Still yourself before HIM and wait and allow HIM to Speak. You may be surprised how much HE has for you. Clean out your Spiritual Ears. Open your Spiritual Eyes. Be Thankful for all that HE has already done in your life because if you wrote it all down, I know it would fill more than just a page. Some of us have a whole Book. Hallelujah! Rejoice in HIM for HE is GOOD! Love, Margene Wiese-Baier July 23, 2015

Father... I Come Before You Today...

Father, I come before you today. First I want to Thank YOU for all YOUR Goodness. I ask today that YOU BLESS EVERYONE on this Page that come together in PRAYER for OTHERS. PRAYER WARRIORS. I ask for each PERSON that NEEDS HEALING, FINANCIAL, LOVE, MARRIAGE, RENEWAL, RELATIONSHIPS, FOR the MINISTRIES, PASTORS, For PEOPLE waiting for DECISIONS that will bring FINANCIAL Security, KNOWING that YOU are OUR PROVIDER and PROVISION. Let everyone FEEL YOUR LOVING EMBRACE. IN JESUS'S NAME. AMEN and AMEN.

HUGS, Margene/Sunwhisp

ENCOURAGE Ourselves...

I was looking in one of my little books that I write in or, should I say, Wrote in. Giving myself little pep talks. Like David, sometimes we have to ENCOURAGE Ourselves.

Excuses, Excuses, Excuses. In why I can't Write or why I can't do my Art. Or why I can't Sing. Come on, Margene. Knock it off. No more Excuses. Get on with what God has for you. Your Destiny is Waiting. Stop listening to People. Listen to God. He is the ONE who Counts. You can Do it Today. Encourage yourself if no one else encourages you. Remember, you have the KING on your Side. HE has your back. Love, Margene

OK...You May Think I Am Strange...and I May Think Differently Than Some of You...

OK, you may think I am Strange, and I may think different than some of you, but sometimes—well OK, Sunday is Mother's Day, and a lot of us are thinking about our Moms. Well, mine like many of yours is now in Heaven. Have you ever thought about how a lot of us are connecting together and have Parents or loved ones that have gone on before us? Hmm. OK. Do you ever think that they are up in Heaven looking down at us and saying to each other, "My child needs your child's help." OK, I told you that you may think that I am Weird or a little Strange, but I don't think that when they go to HEAVEN their work is done. I do look forward to seeing my Mom and Daughter Danielle and other loved ones again and all of my Pets that I had. Please if you still have your Mom, I hope and pray you appreciate her. I know all of you didn't have and Awesome Mom like I did, but if you LOVE your MOM, please let her know. Hugs, and Blessings, Margene

Crossing the Borders from the NATURAL World into the SPIRITUAL WORLD...

Crossing the Borders from the NATURAL World into the SPIRITUAL WORLD. What a JOURNEY we will have. Take the time to get on the Correct Course and DIRECTION that HE has for you. Don't get bogged down into your Circumstances but what you are supposed to be learning from the EXPERIENCE. Start seeing all the Goodness surrounding you. LET your ANGELS know that you have need of them. We have things to do. No time for Sickness, Discouragement, Disharmony with others. Learn to LISTEN with your SPIRITUAL EARS and EYES. HE wants to talk to you today. LISTEN more than talk. HE has a MESSAGE for you today. HEAR HIM. IN JESUS'S NAME. LOVE, Pastor Margene Wiese-Baier

Do Not Share Everything...with Everyone...USE WISDOM...

Do not share everything with everyone. USE WISDOM. Just because someone says they are your friend does not mean they have your best interest in mind or heart. Use your Spiritual Ears and Eyes. Ask God for Discernment. Remember the TRUTH always comes out. You went through certain things for a REASON. Not to HARDEN you, but to show you that when Red flags start waving in your face, take notice, ask questions. Be Blessed to be a Blessing. Love, Pastor Margene Wiese-Baier

Father, I Do Not Understand What Is Going On...

Father, I do not understand what is going on, but I know I am to TRUST YOU. I know that YOU are working behind the SCENES. I know that YOU give us all FREE WILLS and that people can change their minds. So I ask YOU to continue to PROTECT all of my FRIENDS and FAMILY. I ask that YOU make things CLEAR to Me and to keep me on the PATH that I am supposed to be on. I ask for all of those that are supposed to be on this JOURNEY with me to make it CLEAR to them; for those that are not, also make it CLEAR to them. I may not understand today, but YOU know everyone's HEARTS and their TRUE intent toward me. Please OPEN the DOORS that ONLY YOU can OPEN and CLOSE the DOORS that only YOU can CLOSE and help me to WALK away from the ones that have been Closed and WALK through the ONES that I NEED too. I LOVE YOU, LORD, and YOUR NAME of JESUS for you are the ONE that KEEPS me MOVING FORWARD.

LOVE, Margene/Sunwhisp

Sunwhisp FOR the SON that I Worship!

The Waters flow from every stream into rivers, then the vast oceans. Water trickles down the Mountains. Clean and cool and oh so Clear, vibrant and energizing, invigorating. My Spirit Soars as the water pours over me from the waterfall set in the pool of LIFE.

I feel Courage as the words of HIS love are spoken to me. Telling me to come closer. I am mesmerized by HIS Beauty. Sparkling and Translucent like Gold through the Water. I am YOURS and YOU are Mine for all time. Margene/Sunwhisp

Do you have Childlike faith? I pray that you remember the first day that you fell in love with JESUS. It should be the most Wonderful Memory that you have. I don't remember the exact date, but I do know who first told me about HIM. That was my Mother. My Mom was wonderful. Now in Heaven since 1985. It is a wonderful Gift that you can give to your Children. You may not be perfect and you may make a lot of mistakes on the way, but if you can hold on to the LOVE of JESUS, you will be OK and Well. Give the Gift of JESUS today, and remember your Childlike Faith. All is Well in the Name of JESUS. Amen and Amen. Shalom!
Pastor Margene Wiese-Baier

I pray that my LOVE for others is pure. I pray that even when they have hurt me that I do not retaliate as the enemy would want me too, but to react in how My Abba Father would want me to act. In a Godly way of forgiveness and compassion. I ask that God reveals my Heart to others. HE is the one that can judge me. And HE is the one that will fight my battles.

It is hard to do these things, but I would rather that HE protect me from those around me than for me to try to take care of things myself. I have to admit that it might take me some time to realize that the enemy is attacking me. But waking up to knowing that I have HIM that lives within me that is Stronger than he that lives in the World.

Tears comes to my eyes, Knowing how much I am LOVED by the KING. I am the King's Kid and you are too. Seeking HIM always. Love, Margene ♥

Life Is an Adventure!

Life is an Adventure. Enjoy it and look for the Positive side of things. Words are Power, so watch what you say. Treat others as you want to be treated. It will make for a better day. When someone starts putting someone else down, change the subject. Just because they have a problem with that person doesn't mean you will, but use Wisdom. Forgiveness doesn't mean you let people walk all over you, but it is sometimes a time of Pruning. Letting go and letting God! I think one of the most important things I have learned along the way is that we are not made to be friends with everyone. God has the people He wants in our lives, and He will bring them.

Father, I pray that all are encouraged by what was said here. Anything not of you is deleted from their memory, and they only see what you want them to see. In Jesus's Name. Amen and Amen.

Margene/Sunwhisp

Wonderful Councilor. Wonderful Father. Wonderful Creator. All photos taken by Margene Wiese-Baier

Holy Spirit-Inspired Inspirations

Don't give up on your Children or Grandchildren, Natural or Spiritual family. You have a reason that you are in their lives, and they have a reason they are in yours. In this day that people don't know what is going on, HE is the STEADINESS that is needed. KEEP FOCUSED ON HIM AND SEEK HIS KINGDOM. HE IS your ROCK. SHOW them. HE NEEDS TO BE their ROCK TOO. SEEKING SPIRITUAL WISDOM IN ALL THINGS in JESUS CHRIST'S NAME...HALLELUYAH!
Margene Wiese-Baier

I speak LIFE into myself. All exhaustion, Anxiety, and pain must leave my body. I have work to do for the KINGDOM! I do not have time to be in a slumber state. I LOOK above to Abba Father for all my help. I ask that my Angels are dispatched to go ahead of me in all my Journeys. I am Destined with a Plan that HE alone has ordained. People may not understand these things, but the People that do will be for me and not against me. I will walk on water and Soar like the Eagle. I am Triumphant! I am Above and not beneath. I am whom my Father said I am. I do not have to defend myself to anyone because HE already is my defense. My Vindicator. I am Victorious in Jesus's Name. Like liquid gold, he slathers me with HIS Love and gentleness. He will whisper to me all the things HE wants for me. HE has placed in me the Heart of Love. HE has placed in me Compassion for others. HE releases in me all that HE has for me in the right time and the right season.

A Prayer!

Father, there are so many people that are SICK and need your touch. YOUR HEALING POWER. Nothing is too Simple or too Hard for YOU. I also ask for FINANCIAL HELP, especially for those that are Struggling Right now. For those that are trying to do YOUR WORK. I ask for FOOD on their Tables. Clothes on their Backs. ROOFS over Their heads. I ask for Husbands to be at home with their Wives. For Reconciliation between Parents and Children. For Singles to be content and in preparation if they want a Spouse. For Comfort to those that are experiencing some kind of loss. For Endurance for those in Waiting for YOUR PROMISES and to Not give Up. For all to know How much YOU LOVE them. For all things known and unknown. I pray in YOUR SON'S PRECIOUS NAME JESUS. AMEN and AMEN. Love, Margene

It Takes People to Make a Church...

It takes people to make a Church. You don't have to have a Building. You have to have Fellowship. With the Father, Son, and Holy Spirit at the Center, and the Word being Read and lead and for the People to be fed. So the next time someone asks if you are going to Church, remind them you are the Church, and you are going to be in Fellowship. It is not about being inside the Walls, but going out into the Highways and Bi-ways to share HIM with the World. The people inside the Walls already know about HIM. We are called to do more, instead of just getting fat on the word for ourselves, it is time to do something with all that we have been taught. Stop being so selfish and reach out to your fellow man and woman and give them a drink of the Living water, and let them feast on the things that has been stored up in you to spill out onto a Hungry World. Yeshivah is tired of staying a Church building. HE wants to come home with you and go with you wherever you go. You have been poured into to pour out to everyone that you meet. Just a thought or is it?

Margene/Sunwhisp ♥ © 2012

Where Are the SEND-OUT CHURCHES?

Where are the SEND-OUT CHURCHES? Or the Churches that encourage its MEMBERS to not be satisfied just sitting in the PEWS. There are some of us that are not satisfied just warming the seats, but hunger to be MORE, but we do not know where to go and how to get started. If you are wondering why people are getting so frustrated, it is because you are not giving them an OUTLET. PASTORS are like a Father, a Parent, a Teacher, Training a Child on where to go. If you don't help launch them, you are not finishing or doing your job. A Pastor is not called to do it all. Believe it or not, there are people in your congregation that would love to have the opportunity to Serve you. Or looking for a little encouragement to do something that will make a difference. You may have a Billy Graham, a Joyce Meyers, a Kimberly Jones that is bursting at the seams ready to be launched and would love to say that you were the one that helped them to achieve their dreams. Jesus is the Way, they will say, but you were used to help HIM. Wonderful.
Pastor Margene Wiese-Baier

Glorious Expectations. Photo taken by Margene Wiese-Baier © 2012

When a Woman Has Had Enough...She Has Had Enough!

When a Woman has had enough, She has had enough. Sometimes the thing that needs to change is her! Her willingness to wait and see what God wants to do. Did you ever think God is waiting to see how much longer are you (Woman) going to put up with the way he treats you? How much longer are you going to be in DENIAL? Men don't treat a Woman the way he has been treating you. Putting you down. Making threats. Cursing you. How can God bring in the Right man for you as long as you are holding so tightly to what you thought could have been. The man that deserves you will treat you with Respect. Will encourage your gifts and talents. Won't use you just to get ahead. Will love you unconditionally. OK, step back for a Minute. You have to be respectful to him too and treat him well. It is a two-way street. There are some women that don't deserve to be with a good man 'cause they don't know how to treat them. Wake up and smell the Coffee or tea or Roses or whatever. As long as you are still connected. Soul tied to the wrong person as I said God may bring in the Right person, but you won't recognize him till you let go of the one that has been tormenting you. He may even have been the right one in the beginning but opened up the door to allow the enemy to work through him to try to destroy you through Addictions like PORN, Alcohol, drugs. It is time to Allow God to work on things. And really God has been working behind the scenes all along, preparing you for this day of Realizing you are worth so much more. Seek HIM and be Released into your Destiny. MUCHO LOVE, Margene

Don't Let the Enemy Sneak In!

The enemy works overtime on trying to make us feel insecure and take our confidence away. Work hard at not letting him have a crevice to get into, because once he wiggles his way in, he causes more havoc in your life. You have a great opportunity now, and you can see how he tries to cause your Destiny to be Aborted. Allow God to be your guide in Jesus's Name. Love, Margene

Using Your Pain!

Use that PAIN for your GAIN for the TRACTION on your STEPPING-STONE for your FUTURE HAPPINESS. KNOWING WHAT you don't want in a RELATIONSHIP is just HALF the BATTLE in KNOWING WHAT you do want. No more accepting the Trespassers to your HEART; they better have the KEY!
Margene Wiese-Baier

Opening Your Heart!

When you open your HEART to another person, you take the chance of getting HURT. But if you never allowed anyone in, you will never find that One GOD has for you. Listening to the Holy Spirit is the KEY. The RED FLAGS HE sets off inside of you is there for your protection. Allow HIM to give you the GREEN LIGHT. The person that is for you will treat your HEART like it was their OWN!
Margene Wiese-Baier 2015

We were given a HEART To know how other people feel. More importantly to know how GOD feels about that person. Before you speak, check your own heart in how you would feel if they said certain things to you. Words can either encourage or destroy. Remembering the enemy is out to Kill, Steal, and Destroy. Words are like a double-edged sword. Like a child if you only see the mistakes they have made and you only talk to them at that time and forget all the good things they have done. You are more than likely destroying your relationship that you have with them. The same with your other relationships.

If the only thing you received from Abba Father was negative words, you would not continue to talk or listen to HIM. Remember that is not from HIM, but from the enemy. Cherish the Loving Heart HE has given you. When you want to lash back at a person that has hurt you, Allow the Holy Spirit not only heal your heart, but pray for them that they see you only as GOD sees you. HE has a way of making all things that seem so wrong Right again. HE has made you the person you are for a reason.

You are uniquely made. And most of all, HE has qualified you for the Destiny HE is bringing you to. Don't try to be like anyone else. They have to walk their own path to their Destiny, just like you are on your path. Many people may walk beside you for a while, but not all are meant to walk the full distance. The ones that are will not jump ship when you are about to make it but will be there to see you through. Many will help you along the way. Many will be used by the enemy to tell you that you are not what GOD tells you are. The most important things is not to give up. You may think that you are destined for one thing and GOD may even have a bigger plan for you. We never think as BIG as HE does. When no one else encourages you, Encourage yourself like David did.

Love, Margene ♥

David was greatly distressed because the men were talking of stoning him; each one was bitter in spirit because of his sons and daughters. But David found strength in the LORD his God.
1 Samuel 30:6 (NIV)

I am so grateful that God shows me how much HE loves me. HE is the ONE that counts when it comes to everything. Don't let anyone tell you they know what is Best for you. The only ONE that knows what is best for you is your Abba Father. It is not too late for you to go and ask HIM. HIS answer will be positive. The enemy will tell you all the things that are wrong with you. Tell that ole devil and his little irritants that they are liars. One, two, three, tell them to get off at this exit 'cause their ride is over; they can go back to where they came from. Under my feet, Under my feet (from an old song). Love the song, I feel good. God knows you will feel better when you come to the realization that HE is the ONE that has the plan for you. HE is going to place the right people in your life. So stop struggling so much to prove to others that you are worthy of their friendship. Stop explaining and defending your position 'Cause that position maybe the point that God is going to promote you from, and you won't need it anymore. Hope this makes sense. Read Jeremiah. Jesus is the LOVE of my LIFE, HOLDING on tightly to HIM.
Love, Margene 2017 (from my book)

Don't waste your time being Angry with someone. Don't let them have that kind of CONTROL over you. I don't want the Responsibility! And if they are Angry with you, again, don't let them control you. Remember you don't fight against FLESH and BLOOD. The devil loves nothing more than to DISTURB your PEACE. Bumper Cars and Roller Coasters are only fun if they are at an Amusement Park. In Relationships, someone could get hurt. Physical wounds heal, but Mental Scars can last a lifetime. Think before you Speak 'Cause Words do Hurt. Remember your Perception of what is being said is not always the way a person means them. The LEVIATHAN SNAKE will twist your Words. So make sure you make the person understand what you are saying. Is there More to be said?

Love, Margene ♥

Don't Need a Date

Don't be sad if you don't have a date for Valentine's Day! I am not looking just for a Date. Valentine's Day is only One day a year out of my Life. I want a LIFETIME Commitment. Not a One-Night Thrill that will just turn into pain and Guilt. So today is Valentine's Day. Make yourself your Valentine. Do something with friends. There are others out there that are lonely. If we stopped thinking of ourselves, we would be much happier people. Reach out. You never know you may be saving someone's life. Some people don't know how to.

Be a Star, Not a Crab in Someone's Life

I recently wrote a post that had crabs and stars in it. I was talking to a friend yesterday, and she was telling me how one of her friends when she (my friend) wasn't doing well that this person was buddy-buddy with her, but when my friend was doing well would cause trouble in their friendship. She then proceeded to tell me that at a Bible study, she heard to let that person go that is causing strife in your life. You give them two chances then let them go. Wow, pruning time again.

I am a person that I think gives people more than two chances, but sometimes gets burnt and hurt because I tend to love them more then they love me. If that makes any sense.

I know the Father, Son, and Holy Spirit if they weren't forgiving, none of us would have a chance. But are humans different. He is the only One that can change that person. Try though we will, we might hit a brick wall if we try to change someone. Sometimes, we just have to let them go. Sometimes, we get hurt in the process, but we grow from the experience. He sometimes prunes us from relationships so we will grow. As painful as it might be, we sometimes have to let certain people go out of our lives. Because they are poison to our very being. For me, this has been a very hard lesson. The people I thought would be backing me are now gone out of my life for one reason or another. I've had jobs with people that promised me the Moon, but not fulfill a single word they said. I've had friendships deteriorate when I did not bow to their every whim.

If the truth be known, when you make a God connection with someone, they Love you and lift you up in Prayer when the chips are down. They rejoice with you when you are doing well. They cry with you when you need to cry. Hold your hand when you are about to fall. Encourage you when you have had something or someone upset you. They let Jesus talk through them to help show you the way when you have no idea how to get there. Wherever, there is. They listen to you when they are down and know that the Holy Spirit is talking through you. They don't judge you when you're a little off that day. They cover your back when someone or something tries to come against you.

I could go on and on, but I know some of you could add to this. I may not have met you face to face, but there is no Distance in God. All the things I wrote above is how I feel about the people that come onto these pages. I have some personal friends on here that I have met face to face and know that I am loved, encouraged, and we work together to bring Him Glory.

I hope something in here will bless you. Anything not of God disintegrates. Let us all be stars in someone's life. Leave the crabs to be cooked in their own juices. They taste better that way. Sorry, I was thinking of the Crabs you eat. Well anyway, I think you get the gist of what I am talking about.

Handle their life being alone. Be an example of someone that has Jesus living in them. In their life. Healing begins today. Bring it!
Love, Pastor Margene Wiese-Baier ❤️

Who Are You Going to Listen To

Who are you going to listen to: the enemy that is out to kill, steal, or destroy your Destiny or are you going to listen to the Father that knew you before the foundations of the World. It is time we put the enemy under our feet and walk on and leave him in the dust. Yes, I am speaking to you, my child, the one who desperately needs to hear His voice. You need to stop being confused and listen intently to what He wants for you and turn a deaf ear to the enemy. We know His voice. He is talking to you. He wants the best for you. He sees you struggling and wants to bring you higher and higher. Feel His presence; it is good and sweet and lovely. He wraps His arms around you and protects you when you need His protection. Call out His name, Jesus, when the enemy tries to infiltrate your mind and the enemy and his little followers have to flee.

Stop being concerned with the things that He has already told you He is taking care of. Our families, our friends, and the relationships even in the future. He has it all under control. (I am talking to myself here too.) Margene, are ya listening? The insecurities and the loneliness we all have felt, the enemy tries to use them to defeat us, but we have a Big God that can handle that little guy. He is nothing, but Our God is something.

Be encouraged; we have Angels fighting our battles for us. And I am thankful that God sent us a Comforter called the Holy Spirit. That I can do anything with Him covering me.

Be Satisfied and not Petrified in what He has called you to do. Just listened to TD Jakes and even he was shaking and couldn't hold the microphone when he first started. And as Joyce always says, "Do it Afraid." She did and many more that have been called by His name have done it afraid too.

Come on, People, we have work to do. The World is drowning in the misconception that anything goes and that God accepts everything. It just isn't so; read John in the Bible, and it answers a lot of questions people have and for some of us who feel too intimidated to answer can say, but it is there in black and white. So when people try to push you in the corner, you don't have to defend yourself, but direct them to the Bible where all the answers are, then when they say they don't like what you say, you can tell them, "I am not the one who said it, but it is written in black and white, read it for yourself."

We are living to the effect that without Him, we would not have seen the victories in our lives. We need to be bold and tell others about the things He has brought us through. What can they say—You're a liar. Well, you know the truth, and you know what you went through, and most of the time, there has been witnesses to your testimony that God placed these people to back you up. If you know me very well, you know I hate confrontation. I can stand up for any sister or brother, but have a hard time standing up for myself. That is why we were put in relationship to not only stand up for each other, but to stand beside each other in this battle we call life. And most of all, Stand Up for What We Believe!

I pray for all of you that you are and have been blessed today by what was written, but also that you gain the boldness to step out into what God has called you to do. Standing together we can bring Love and happiness and encouragement to the World not for us, but to Glorify Our King and Savior, Jesus Christ. Yeshua (sp)

Blessings and Hugs, Margene

Sunday, I listened to Dutch Sheets, and he talked about how sometimes he would feel so depressed and didn't know why he felt so bad. Then it dawned on him that he was being attacked.

Spiritual Attacks are real. They can be devastating. I am sure glad when God shows us that HE is always with us.

HE has given us the Authority to dispatch our Angels and to tell the enemy to flee. The Blood of Jesus is our answer.

I am learning that what we have is what the enemy wants. He will attack us where we are most vulnerable. Put on your Armor.

Love is the Answer. Learning that we do not have to put up with the enemy's attacks is crucial. Learning how to detect when we are being attacked is very important. Having friends that will pray for us when we can't is essential.

Love you all in Jesus.
Psalm 91 King James Version
He that dwelleth in the secret place of the most High shall abide under the shadow of the Almighty.
I will say of the Lord, He is my refuge and my fortress: my God; in him will I trust.
Surely he shall deliver thee from the snare of the fowler, and from the noisome pestilence.

He shall cover thee with his feathers, and under his wings shalt thou trust: his truth shall be thy shield and buckler.

Thou shalt not be afraid for the terror by night; nor for the arrow that flieth by day;

Nor for the pestilence that walketh in darkness; nor for the destruction that wasteth at noonday.

A thousand shall fall at thy side, and ten thousand at thy right hand; but it shall not come nigh thee.

Only with thine eyes shalt thou behold and see the reward of the wicked.

Because thou hast made the Lord, which is my refuge, even the most High, thy habitation;

There shall no evil befall thee, neither shall any plague come nigh thy dwelling.

For he shall give his angels charge over thee, to keep thee in all thy ways.

They shall bear thee up in their hands, lest thou dash thy foot against a stone.

Thou shalt tread upon the lion and adder: the young lion and the dragon shalt thou trample under feet.

Because he hath set his love upon me, therefore will I deliver him: I will set him on high, because he hath known my name.

He shall call upon me, and I will answer him: I will be with him in trouble; I will deliver him, and honour him.

With long life will I satisfy him, and shew him my salvation.

Psalm 23 King James Version, "The Lord is my shepherd; I shall not want. He maketh me to lie down in green pastures: he leadeth me beside the still waters.

He restoreth my soul: he leadeth me in the paths of righteousness for his name's sake.

Yea, though I walk through the valley of the shadow of death, I will fear no evil: for thou art with me; thy rod and thy staff they comfort me.

Thou preparest a table before me in the presence of mine enemies: thou anointest my head with oil; my cup runneth over.

Surely goodness and mercy shall follow me all the days of my life: and I will dwell in the house of the Lord for ever and ever.

And remember Jeremiah 29:11, "For I know the plans I have for you," declares the Lord, "plans to prosper you and not to harm you, plans to give you hope and a future."

Let us soar like the Eagle.

Put on some Praise Music and Worship HIM. Learn how to be quiet and truly listen for HIS voice. HE whispers.

The enemy is out to Kill, steal, and destroy. God is out to RESTORE. HALLELUYAH! Love, Margene/Sunwhisp ❤ ♥ From my book 2017

I Believe!

I Believe!

John 3:16-17 "For God so loved the World that He sent His only Begotten Son that whosoever believes in Him will not perish but have everlasting Life. For God did not send His Son into the world to condemn the world, but that the world through Him might be saved."

I am a Supernatural being having a Human experience. To just be Human would be boring.

I believe there is a God that is here to help us, and I believe there is an enemy that is here to torment us.

I believe there is a Heaven and a Hell. They are both very real.

I believe that God sent His Son, Jesus, to die and be raised from the dead and to go back to Heaven to sit at His right side so I can go to Heaven myself one day.

I believe He knew me before the very foundation of the World and that He mapped out a Plan and a Purpose for my Life. As it is said in Jeremiah 29:11.

I believe He renews my strength and my youth like the Eagle.

I believe He is my King of Everything.

I believe He is the One True God.

I believe without Him, I am nothing. With Him, I am a son or daughter of The Most High God.

I believe He is my source and My Provision. He will show me how to gain Wealth. I will ask for Wisdom and all things will be added on.

I believe He works through me to do good and not harm. He is merciful, so I must be merciful to others. He forgives me, so I must forgive others.

If I am ashamed of Him, he will be ashamed of me. I want to stand on His word. To encourage and to tell others of His Love for them. I do not need to argue about my faith, He has my back.

I will not be double-minded. I will not have two masters. I cannot serve Him and serve manna. He is the only one I will follow and no other.

In March, when I was down on the ground after catching my shoe in the crack of the sidewalk, I asked God if He wanted to take me home, and I said I would go, but if He still had work for me to do, I was willing to stay. Well, I am still here, so I guess I still have work to do.

It has been a little rough since then, and sometimes I have to admit I would have rather gone home to Heaven and look down upon others struggling in the World. That would have been the easy way. But He has a Plan and a Purpose for my life that needs to be fulfilled. He shows me over and over how He takes care of me in little things, and sometimes things that just blow my mind. That no way I could even imagine how to work them out on my own.

Things happening that no man could make happen.

So if I seem stubborn and committed to only one God, The only God that has a son named Jesus that was sent to earth to die for us. When Jesus went back to Heaven, He sent us the comforter the Holy Spirit.

Then so be it. I want to be that person that is the "Apple of His Eye," His little Princess. Letting His light shine through me is my Goal in life. I like the thought that there is something (Someone) bigger than myself helping me.

And yes, even knowing when something goes wrong in my life, it isn't always my humanness that has caused it, but an enemy that is out to kill, steal, and try to destroy me. I like the thought that there is something (Someone) bigger than myself helping and protecting me. Sending His Angels to encamp around me. Giving me a Guardian Angel that has been with me since birth.

God does not condemn but pricks the Heart to love Him. He first loved me and invited me to be His daughter. I accepted the invitation. I can't say it has been a party since then, but I can be a testimony to others to help in their times of struggle. (I loved Jesus since a little girl.) My loving Mother told me about Him when I was very young. Both of my parents were believers, and I am so thankful for that.

So Yes, I am a Supernatural Being having a Human experience, and it definitely hasn't been boring having a Loving Heavenly Father that has a Plan and a Purpose for my Life.

I hope this encourages you to stand firm on your belief in Him. He has a Plan and a Purpose for your life. 2010 is the year that His Promises to you will come to pass.

Just a thought! Or is it?

Love and Blessings and a Big Hug, Margene

PS: Read the story about Thomas in John 20:29.

Mathew 8:5-10 The story about the Roman Centurion.

How We React!

The last couple of days, I have been doing a lot of thinking and praying about why we do the things we do. Especially when it comes to eating and the way we keep our houses. And the way everything connects together.

Some people when they are stressed go and find something to eat. For some, it is something sweet like a chocolate chip cookie or should I say cookies. For some, it is something salty like a bag of barbeque potato chips. Remember, you can't eat just one. And then there are the people that go crazy and clean an already clean house. And then there are some of us that when we get stressed, we become immobile and our houses show it. And then there are the people that are combo people that everything mentioned is happening to them.

Have you ever been to someone's house that you swear you could eat off their floor, and then the next time you drop in, things just aren't the same? Well, did you ever question that something just might be going on in their World? Or a person that has been thin and then the next time you see them, you swear they must have gained twenty pounds. Or it may be the opposite.

Well, we all have something that we are going through and each of handle it in different ways.

I can remember when a friend's Mother passed on. My friend lost so much weight, she became skin and bones. Her face was shallow and sunken in, and she just didn't look like her anymore. And the Father/Husband did the same thing. A robust little man with a little round belly turned into a thin man almost like overnight.

I also have friends that would react to a situation differently. They eat everything in sight. Food is their comfort barometer. Even though they are full, they have to finish the whole bag of cookies.

Or let's look at the people that all of a sudden or not so suddenly can't keep their house clean. Did you ever wonder what is going on there. Or even worse when it is a struggle all along. For myself, I think it goes deeper than just looking at what is going on the surface. It goes to the root or the core of the person. Recently, we had a woman come into Fisherman's Net that taught on Bitter Root Judgments. I believe in each of these situations something happened in the past to make us react a certain way. For the friend and her Dad that lost the weight, you can see it was a traumatic experience right then. But what about the others? And maybe even with the friend and her Dad what happened to them long ago to make them react the way they did by not being able to eat. The problem is when people go back to eating, their body says you starved me long enough. I am going to store the fat away, so if you ever do it again, I will have reserves.

In a couple days, it is a start of a New Year of 2010. Time of trying to better ourselves in the New Year. I think before we can make improvements, we need to look at why we do certain things. God wants us to be the best we can be and wants us to come to Him for help. Most of us have tried to carry everything on our own shoulders for way to long. He can show us where and why and the reasons we do the things we do. We need to stop blaming others and be forgiving if someone else caused you not to feel good about yourself. Especially when it comes to parents; they did the best they could. They may not have felt loved when they were children and just don't know how to show love. Or it could be something that happened with someone at School. The teasing that went on and then they would say it is because we like you. Well, you know it didn't feel like you liked me. Words hurt more than if you would have thrown something. I think you get my point.

Sometimes, if you notice someone is doing something they normally don't do or even if you notice, it is a pattern. Can you do me a favor? Open the door for that friend to voice what is going on. Don't tell others unless you have that person's permission. You may just be the window that person needs to be a healing into their hurting soul.

I was talking to one of my friends, and she said every part of us including our body has been hurt by something. It truly shows in how we keep our house and how we eat our food. I pray I have not offended anyone because I want to write in love, and by writing this, helps me also into seeing why I react to things in a certain way.

Please tell me if this has helped you. Or tell me how you have overcome certain things in your life. By doing this you can help someone else.

Just a thought! Hugs and Love, Margene

PS: I am glad I have someone bigger than myself to bring me through the tough times. Just because I am a Believer in Jesus Christ doesn't mean I will not go through trials and tribulation. It even says that in the Bible. But I do know who my Comforter is, and He is always there to get me through anything. 2010 is a turnaround year. I believe the Promises made will be fulfilled this year. Get Ready, Get Ready, Get Ready. Just a thought! Hugs, Margene

Write a comment.

Slim for Him, This Book Made a Difference

I saw a friend that I hadn't seen for some time, and she looked marvelous, dawling. She had lost about seventy pounds, and I was so excited for her. I asked her how she did it, and she proceeded to tell me, and she told me about a book another friend had given her and how it impacted her life. I was with this friend when she bought the book at the Fisherman's Net bookstore in North Port after a Woman's Bible study. She picked up the book and told me she was going to buy it for a certain friend. It cost her a whole 25 cents. If this little book can help my friend, maybe it can help others. I want to share it with all of my friends and family. It is an older book and I don't know if it is available, but for those who have connections, please help me find it. I hope this is a blessing for you. The book is Slim for Him, and the author is Patricia B Kreml. Please let me know what you think. Love and hugs, Margene

Serving Others a Great Present to Give, but I Get More in Return Than What I Gave!

I am so excited. I had a Wonderful Christmas where I could give to others, and guess what? It was a Christmas meal. I helped several other people serve the Homeless in Fort Myers. So excited. It reminded me of

the days I went with Team Jesus, and Bill and Charlene Cameron would have been cheering me on.

My friend came and picked me up Christmas Eve, so we could get an early start in the morning. She was gracious to me and let me sleep until 8:00 a.m. instead of six. She didn't know I got up several times because I didn't want to hold up anything.

We drove to Fort Myers, and this is how good God is: the very things we had talked about the night before and that morning was on a TD Jakes CD. I swear confirmation all over that CD. Powerful. Then we got there and a crowd of people were there waiting. Oh man, you should have seen the spread. Chicken, Pork Ribs so tender and juicy. Mashed potatoes with garlic and butter. Vegetables sautéed in butter and herbs. Lasagna like from Italy itself. And then the desserts. I swear it was like we were serving Royalty. Kind of reminds me of the story when the big guys were invited to the Wedding, and they were too busy to come. But the people that were meant to be there came. It was beautiful. The babies, the men, and the women. Smiles and laughter filled the air. I went around taking pictures of all these beautiful people. That for one day they could forget all of their problems and enjoy not only a good meal, but other people's company in conversation and laughter.

Yesterday, we celebrated our King's birth, but He didn't stay a baby. He grew up to lay down His life to save us from destruction. He died for us and rose again and sits at the right hand of His Father. But yesterday, as we served others, He walked amongst the people and blessed them in a special way.

I wouldn't have missed this for the World. I look forward to next year and doing it again. Oh wait, I don't think I will have to wait. Pastor Gasper Anastasi invited us to come back New Year's Eve. I think he said we could help again. Okay, when we do something like this, we sometimes think we are blessing others, but the truth is we are the one getting the blessing. I feel all warm and comfy inside. I Love you, Jesus, and You make my world Rock with Joy, and I feel Loved so much by you when I can serve others as You have served me.

Just a thought. Or is it?
Love, and Hugs, Margene

Grandma and a Man We Called Doc

As I entered the train station in Albany, Oregon, my eyes automatically focused on an older gentleman. If he wasn't a man, I would have sworn my grandmother had come back to take this life-changing trip with me, but she was in Heaven. It did cause the memories of the long-ago trips of my youth to see her and her husband who we all called Doc.

It would always be the same scenario. Dad would come home on Fridays after a long hard working day at his Saw Filing Shop, where he sharpened big saws for the local lumber mills in Philomath, Oregon, and a few on the outskirts of the town.

His announcement was always "Hurry up, and get ready. We're going to see Grandma." Before we could go, we had to make sure the house was cleaned up. That kind of ruined the spontaneity of the trip, but it didn't ruin the excitement of going. We always made sure the house was spotless because Mom would remind us that nothing was worse than coming home to a dirty house, and it was a nice to slip into clean, crisp sheets after the long drive home. I could never figure how it always seemed like it took forever to get to a place and just half the time to get home.

Off we went for the drive that seemed to always bring up the same question over and over again: "Are we there yet?" With the resounding same answer," Not yet, but it won't be long now."

We would finally get there after what seemed like an eternity, even though we had slept most of the way, in between the squabbling that sisters and brothers do because they're bored out of their gourd.

Grandma and Doc and sometimes my Uncle John would come out to greet us, with gigantic grins on their faces. They seemed just as excited to see us as we were in seeing them. We seemed to fall out of the car because we had car lag from being confined for far too long, but being kids, we didn't feel the effect long.

The first thing we wanted to do was see the goats, and we hoped for some new baby kids to pet. Doc always had a fun way to call them, and I swear he sounded just like one of them Baaaaaa! BAAAA! BAAAA!

It seemed we were starving by the time we got there, so we anxiously went into the house, which always had the scent of Grandma in every nook and cranny. Not a sweet smell or even a sour citrus smell, but a unique Grandma smell that made us feel all warm inside because if we could smell that fragrance, we knew that we were loved.

Grandma's smell had to compete with the sensational smells of the roast beef cooking in the oven. It always had fresh carrots, potatoes, onions, garlic, right out of the garden depending on what time of the year it was. If we were lucky, Uncle John gathered mushrooms in the woods that morning. It was a delight to our noses as the juices combined to entice us with their luscious fragrance that had been simmering most of the day.

Then the tantalizing bread that had just been baked, fresh from the oven, a combination of nuts, different grains, anything Grandma could think of that would make her bread unique and flavorful. It was always crispy on the outside, tender on the inside, generously sliced with gobs of goat's butter and possibly cheese, sweet honey, and even homemade strawberry or blueberry jam if the mood hit us to explore our taste buds.

Of course, there was always ice-cold goat's milk and Doc always proposed the question, "Do you like goat's milk?" and we gave the resounding answer, "Yeeeeeeeees!" We were pretty good imitators, but Doc had taught us this from the first time we met. For dessert, we weren't quite sure if we'd like it because Grandma always experimented with the goat's milk. She tried her hand at ice cream and sometimes came up with some pretty strange concoctions. Sometimes we didn't even know what to say because we didn't want to hurt her feelings, but yuck! Some of it was gross, and we couldn't even eat it without having an uncontrollable urge to upchuck. Sometimes though, she'd come up with something good like peach ice cream, so we'd try it even though we knew that we might be making a mistake.

After we were totally stuffed and wanting to roll out the door because our stomachs seemed to moan, "You fed me far too much!" My two brothers, sister, and I would go outside to have a little adventure of our own, while the grownups stayed in the house to visit.

Adventures on Grandma's farm were fun for us, because not living on a farm, we could roam freely without the confines of streets and concrete sidewalks. The dirt was either hot or cool depending whether we were under numerous trees in the woods or standing in an open field. We had to watch out for the stinky old billy goat because we were warned that he liked to butt you. The rank putrid old goat had horns, too, so we didn't want to test his ornery moods by getting in his area of the pasture. We hoped some kind of fence was between him and us protecting our tender backsides.

Doc sometimes came out with us because he liked to tell us stories of the good ole days when he grew up and his adventures as a traveling salesman. We never tired of his stories because he told a story so entertainingly that we felt we were there wherever there was. His stories were better than fairytales because we knew they were real, and it made us closer every time he shared another little part of himself with us.

My favorite story he would tell us is about his family living in a small cabin in the woods at the bottom of Mt. St. Helens. The farmers and town folk nicknamed old Mt. St. Helens Madcap because they never knew when she would blow. The mountain was festering up something because every once in a while, people would say they could hear her rumbling and making all sorts of weird noises. Stories abounded how the volcano would erupt again someday. Doc told of this old man named Truman that swore he would never leave even if Old Madcap blew. Doc told us about his sister Anne that sat on the fence gate and yodeled to her audience of cows and a bull named King Alfred. Her ambition in life was to grow up and be a cowgirl and ride in the rodeos. His parents gave Doc his nickname because he nursed every sick animal back to health. He had that special combination of love and intuition that gave him the insight to know exactly what kind of herbs would cure the poor critters. One day, a traveling salesman came by his family's cabin selling different concoctions promising to cure anything from the common cold to Scarlet Fever. The man had everything on his wagon that a person would every need. From that day, Doc decided that that is what he wanted to be. He began dreaming from that day of the adventures that he would have traveling from town to town. He told us that it disappointed his parents, but his dreams came true. It sure made good stories to tell us—his grandchildren.

All aboard. It was time to go. I grabbed my bags and took Charlie (small dog) and put her under my arm and boarded the train. It was time to start my adventure. Doc would be proud. I knew that throughout the trip to Florida, I would continue to visit memory lane where I would meet Grandma and the man we called Doc.

Indecision/Decision

It's confusing when you're trying to make a decision that is going to change your life forever. When you finally make that decision and stick with it is like having the feeling of complete triumph, that a weight, like a two-ton elephant, has been lifted off your shoulders. The sticking with it is the hard part. Especially when you have friends and family that don't want you to change.

When I decided to get a divorce, so much life got in the way it took years to finally go through with the process. Was it life or fear? Being afraid of losing my children. Wow, what a revelation. I had forced that one back into the storage banks of my mind. You know the part where you put things you really don't want to deal with because to deal with them would be far too painful. My kids were my life. Afraid that I would be making a huge mistake because he really was a pretty good guy, wasn't he?

Just because my self-esteem was nonexistent and just because I felt no one else would love and accept me the way I was like he did.

He needed me. I was there to help him, save him. Save him from what? Being an alcoholic, from self-destructing? Combusting and going completely mad? Going through Milestones Alcohol Treatment Center with him was pure Hell for me. Having to listen to how bad he felt for

159

all his other girlfriends in how he had treated them. What about me? Wasn't I the one who was his wife and the mother of his children? For God's sake! What about me? Thank God! He finally sought the help of the VA (Veterans) to help him get over the hurdle of being in Vietnam. I did not want to even try to fathom the horror of being in a war that no one wanted to support, let alone come to terms with, and acknowledge that it really happened, but like the alcohol treatment, I stuck with him through all the pain of flashbacks, and nightmares. The sad whimpering like a sad puppy when he was having a nightmare. Waking him, assuring him that it was only a bad dream and that no one was chasing him. I didn't want to hear what the dream was about, because I didn't want to relive his horror in my own dreams.

What I found is no one can save you; you have to save yourself. Once I found that truth, the decision to get a divorce was easy. Besides I needed to save myself, and I wouldn't be able to do that in the confines of and unhealthy, unloving marriage. Inside ourselves, we have an image and ideal of what a happy marriage should look like, and my marriage didn't even come close to my internal perception of what that would be. The worst thing about being in a bad relationship is that you can't give your children a good example of what a good, loving, healthy relationship should look and feel like.

I guess that is my biggest regret about not making the decision sooner is that I could have possibly gotten into a healthy relationship. It seemed every time I tried to get out of the marriage before, my children would talk me into staying. They would do this even though they were the ones that would tell me, "Divorce Dad, because he's so mean to you." Wow, what the human heart does to contradict itself to stay in the familiar. Love has always been important to me, and I always wondered why I couldn't love this man, but how easy it was to love the children we created together.

I yearned to be with my soul mate and came to the tearful conclusion that this man wasn't him. Not only was I sad for myself at this revelation, but I was sad for him because I knew he deserved to be with someone that loved and cherished him, and I knew I could no longer try to be that person, and I knew I deserved the same for myself. It's amazing how the minutes, hours, and oh yes, the years just pass in a blink of an eye. A speck of time in the scheme of things. Here I was at my wedding not knowing if I was doing the thing. Even though I had a gut-wrenching feeling that I should not be going through with it, but then I said to myself, "If it happens, it must be meant to be." A decision not to make a decision is the worst decision of all because the decision usually turns out to be the wrong one.

That feeling long ago while standing in front of the minister when God was telling me I shouldn't marry this man. Maybe He was really telling me that this is just a small part of your life because if I wouldn't have gone through with the marriage, I wouldn't have had two beautiful daughters and a beautiful grandson that took twenty-one years to come into existence. What could be more gratifying than bringing life to children that could possibly make all your wrong decisions right just by being.

So why did God give us a brain anyway just to let life happen to us or for us to make our lives the best we can. Now I know it is our duty as human beings to use or intelligence God gave us to make good decisions. If we really listen, He will even help us. It may be that gut -wrenching feeling, a friendly word whispered in our ear, a gentle tug at a corner of our heart, or that nagging little thought that runs helter-skelter through the recesses of our minds. Life is a learning experience. I hope I learned what I needed to learn, and now I have a second chance.

Not a chance: to go back and change the past, but the chance to change the future into something that I can be proud of. Regrets are futile and not worth my energy. I am ready to fulfill my destiny; I hope I will do something that will leave a loving imprint on all humanity. Or at least I know that from now on my decisions will be the right decisions, so I can continue my saga of life in dignity.

America Land of the Beautiful and Free?
Freedom in America: Fact or Fiction!

From the foundation of America's existence, people from every nation of the world have made it their home because of the belief. That in America, every individual would have Religious freedom and every opportunity to become successful.

Lay a hand on America—Wrong! That's what Americans once thought before the tragedy that took place September 11, 2001. America's enemies have been filtering in for years, and as a good neighbor, America has unintentionally let it happen. It is time to get a handle on the situation and do something about the influx of the enemy. Joining forces with other nations against terrorism could be the key to bring America back to where it should be. Getting back on their knees before God was the best course of action taken. The enemy is not a majority of people from a different culture, but a minority of misguided individuals. As Americans, it is essential that fact be recognized; therefore, innocent people are not persecuted for the wrongs of the guilty. Authors will write about this tragic event for many years to come because it shook the nation.

Since the tragic event that brought the World Trade Center down, America has had to buckle down and get serious in an unserious society. People who thought only of themselves are now looking at the needs of their fellow man. Getting God back in the scenario was the first step in healing this great nation. America, please do not take a step backward and kick Him out again. In the great speech "I Have a Dream," Martin Luther King Jr. said, "With this faith we will be able to work together; to pray together, to struggle together, to go to jail together, to stand up together, knowing that we will be free one day. This will be the day when all of God's children will be able to sing with new meaning, 'My country 'tis of thee; sweet land of liberty; of thee I sing; land where my fathers died, land of the pilgrim's pride; from every mountain side, let freedom ring.'" People need to remember what America's forefathers had in mind when they said, "All men are created equal." This great nation was not created for a select few, but for every color and race. Working together, citizens can make the United States an even better place to call home, where freedom can be embraced. It can be a place where threats from terrorists will not be tolerated, but dealt with immediately, so America will never have to endure another 9/11 event.

A string of events happened before that shook America's faith (Y2K, Pearl Harbor Attack, Oklahoma City Bombing), but nothing made the people tremble in fear, as the events that occurred that day. The lasting impression of September 11 forever changed life, as Americans knew it and America would never be viewed in the same way. Out of desperation, America sought the God of the Christian faith to help heal the nation. Even though God did not cause the September 11 tragedy, He allowed it to happen because of man's free will. Christians around the World kept saying, "What the Evil One meant for evil, God will turn it around for good." All Americans will remember 9/11, as the pivotal point in the twenty-first century (and know there would be no turning back to the way it used to be). Authors will continue to write about this tragic event for centuries to come because of how it shook this great nation.

The land of the free and the beautiful has been tarnished forever. Although this may be true, this great nation has never been more unified, making it the best place on this planet to live. Let Freedom Ring.

I Must Be About My Father's Business

I must be about my Father's Business—This is what I live by. I wanted to share with family and friends one of my accomplishments. This came right in time to lift my Spirit. When I feel a little down, God has a way of sending me someone or something to get me back on track. Someone told me the other day that my attitude changed. I am glad because I was pitiful. I thank all the people that have been keeping me lifted up in prayer; it means a lot to me. I feel truly loved. I want the best for my fellow man and want them to know the truth about the man, Jesus, because without Him I would not be here. Love and Blessings, and of course lots of Hugs.

Margene

PS: I am tired of just thinking about me, but I do really want to be about His business and that means caring and loving other people. There are so many out there lost and hopeless, and it is time for us to reach out a hand to them and help them get back up. If that just means a simple smile or whatever God shows us to do. So be it. I am ready and willing to get down to business. I am open to what He has destined me to do before the foundations of the World. Jeremiah 29:11 So are ya listenen!

MARGENE WIESE-BAIER

I Must be about My Father's Business
Across the street or Across the sea
I must Go
I must show
My Father's Heart
Where shall I start
Across the street or Across the sea
Which one shall It be
I am but the vessel that He must fill
Let me overflow me and let me spill
Across the street or Across the sea

Benevolence...Honduras

Benevolence...Honduras
Men Women Children
Crying Shattered Hearts
Childhood to Horrible to Remember
Curses Broken
Love Unspoken
The Father's Heart
A Place to Start
Love Rekindled
Hope Un-spindled
A Boy's Prison A Children's Park
Each Very Dark
Let Me be the Spark that Ignites the fire
that starts the Heart to Love Again

MARGENE WIESE-BAIER

DON'T WAIT TILL TOMORROW - DO IT TODAY

DON'T WAIT TILL TOMORROW
DO IT TODAY
IF YOU HAVEN'T SAID YES TO JESUS
DON'T DO IT TOMORROW, DO IT TODAY
IF YOU HAVEN'T ASKED FOR FORGIVENESS
DON'T IT TOMORROW, DO IT TODAY
IF YOU HAVENT SAID I LOVE YOU
DONT DO IT TOMORROW, DO IT TODAY
TOMORROW MAY NOT COME SO
DONT WAIT TILL TOMORROW, DO IT TODAY

Marriage

I look in a floor-length mirror that holds tomorrow.

I'm about to get married, not a young giddy bride, but years older and wiser.

Putting my past behind to start a new adventure.

My white lace veil covers my eyes, but I can see.

My shoulders are caressed with fine silk and my skin enjoys the touch of its gentleness.

I see the strength and wisdom that brought me to this place in my life.

I coo to myself as if in a trance ready for flight in readiness to soar to new heights like an eagle.

I am that eagle ready to meet my mate.

Ready to start our life together.

Ready to build a nest softened with the down of our feathers.

Branch by branch, we will intertwine our foundation together.

We will talk of love to each other through our beaks.

A love song will engage our every movement.

We will enjoy our oneness and want to be together for all eternity.

We will soar together in perfect harmony.

We will see nothing but beauty surrounding us.

The mountains capped with the purity of snow.

The frosted trees after a refreshing rain, holding tightly to their leaves to protect all that they hold beneath them.

The earth covered with pine needles and soft sod that with hold the footprints of all who walk there.

The lakes below of crystal blue ecstasy with tongues of water lapping at their beaches.

The buffalo that thunders across the plains thankful to be forgotten by the hunters of yesteryear.

The coyote plays with her kits and waits patiently for the return of her mate. Brother Elk watching his harem bathing in a nearby lake.

We land to refresh ourselves in the coolness of a mountain stream, and I look in and see my reflection and see the promises of tomorrow.

Hunger All Around

Tragic but true it is nothing new. Hunger is all around.
People do not need to be in a War to feel their stomachs roar.
People do not need to be homeless to feel the pangs of pain that hunger brings. It could be a neighbor that a person needs to feed.
For hunger is all around us.
Unfortunate but true, so what can this one person do.

Forgiveness. Broken Bones Heal Faster Than Hurtful Words

Do you remember when you were a kid that you could get mad at your best friend or brother or sister, and the next day, it was all forgotten and you played together like nothing happened. My Mom and Dad would not have to say or interfere because they knew this would happen. Even when I became a parent to my two wonderful daughters and had to discipline them for one reason or another, they would rush up to me afterward and give me a big hug and say I love you Mommy, and tell me I am sorry for not listening to you. I see my relationships with others now that I am a grown woman that I need to nurture those relationships just like I did when I was a child and forgive others when they hurt me. My Mom used to say, "Sticks and Stones may break my bones, but words may never hurt you." Wrong, thankfully it was just a saying, because words hurt worse than a broken bone. Recently, I fell and was hurt, but am being healed daily, but the words that some people have said to me have cut me like a knife. By the grace of God, I can and will forgive those people. Maybe, they don't even know that they hurt me. I want to be like that child of long ago and forgive and go on like nothing happened. I will do my part, now it is up to them to do their part. Is it not because I am the bigger person No! It is because I have the One in me that has forgiven me for all the things I have done that hurts Him.

Forgiveness is a precious gift our Father gave us but is something we can give freely to each other if we just open our hearts.

I hope this touches something in your Heart and a healing begins for those that feel hurt by others. Remember, it isn't them it is the enemy working through them that wants to Kill, Steal, and Destroy. The Devourer. I am glad that we have someone bigger in our lives that has come to Heal the Broken Hearted, and His name is Jesus. Hugs, Margene

Dance with Me, Lover of My Soul/ Time to Come Forward

I am talking to those that have felt that tugging at their heartstrings to go forward and worship, but have been hindered in some way. Oh, I am shy, I am quiet. I don't know how to dance. That just isn't me. Well no, it isn't you, it is something inside of you that wants to press in and get everything that He has for you. To look up and to get into His presence and to exalt Him. I want everyone to feel the excitement that I am feeling. Can you imagine if everyone went forward in one accord, what would happen? What could happen? Wowser! Wowser! Wowser! What joy it would bring to our King. To have everyone unite in one body and give Him all the glory. Why is it we do not have any trouble going forward when the Pastor does an Altar call for something we need or want from our Father, but it is so hard to get out of our seats to go Worship Him. It saddens my heart to think that we are so self-centered. We are not just part of one church, but God is sending us out to other places. We are to bring the light, we are to bring the Worship. When we go into another Church, people should notice that there is something different about us. We don't go forward to worship to say look at me, I am special, but to get into His presence. To bring Him all the Glory, and if we can help bring others into His presence how cool is that. Father, let me be the one to let your light shine through me a beacon that radiates your love. To give a hug and let my arms be your arms around that person. To give a smile that radiates your love through my lips. To lay hands on them in healing, knowing it isn't me that is doing the healing, but you working through my vessel. For I am only an instrument to be used by You.

Dance with me, oh Lover of my soul. That song just keeps reigniting in my mind and heart. All He asks is that you come dance with Him. I remember when I first started going to Suncoast Worship Center. I said to God this is so weird. He told me to shut my eyes and He would show me how to worship Him. Stop looking at everyone else and how they are worshiping. The next thing I knew, I was up front dancing. At that time, there were several people dancing up front. This was the old Sanctuary. A lot of Glory Holes in that place and it felt like an Open Heaven. Such Freedom. I pray that for the building that we are in now. The chains of bondage broken off. We sing the song Freedom, but do we really have it? Are we really living it? Or are we squelching the things He has for us by not obeying Him when He asks us to go forward. Maybe some of us need a little help and encouragement from our fellow members. So we have two left feet. God is not looking at our feet, but our heart. When we sing, it may sound to us like a person that is tone deaf, but God sees the person's heart and it is truly beautiful to Him. It is anointed and may bring someone to Worship Him also. We use the scenario about being at a Football game and yelling for our team, why can't we make a joyful noise for Our Father, but I never heard the one about going to the Nightclubs and dancing in the world, why not dance for Jesus until Bonnie said it in the Communion with God class. Wowser, what a revelation!

I was at Deep Creek Worship Center, and God had Judy down on the floor, and He confirmed everything I am saying here. Maybe in our younger years, we went out dancing in the World. Dance and Singing are just some of the things that are really gifts given to be used in the Church.

I am just so excited to see what God is doing in many of our lives. Especially when it is happening in my own life. There are a lot of things that are still in process of course, but what a process. What a joy to be living in a time such as this. Wow, so Awesome. I get anxious sometimes because God's timing is not my timing, but He has never failed me. The answers are not always the answers I am expecting. His ways are always better than my ways.

I can't wait to see what He does next.

Sunwhisp's Notes and Quotes and Art to Inspire and bring Glory to Jesus's Fan Box

I am a Christian that does as much Ministry work as possible. I am working on myself to be the best person I can be.

We as Christians need to STAND UP FOR WHAT WE BELIEVE IN. NON-CHRISTIANS DON'T SEEM TO HAVE ANY TROUBLE DOING IT. IT IS TIME FOR US TO SHOW THAT WE HAVE A KING BEHIND US AND THAT WE ARE THE KING'S KIDS. Just so tired of others pushing us around, but the trouble is we let them. If we would all just read the BIBLE, we would see that JESUS didn't put up with anything. HE only did when HE was going to the CROSS, AND THAT IS BECAUSE HE WAS GIVING HIS LIFE FOR US. BUT LOOK, HE ROSE UP AND LIVED AGAIN. I believe HE is proud of us when we Stand up and say what HE gives us. I know that what I say. I pray it is HOLY SPIRIT INSPIRED. I know my Mom now in HEAVEN IS PROUD OF Me too. I am all about love on my personal page and my Ministry pages, but when I was praying and talking to Abba Father about this and said, but I am about Love. HE showed what more is LOVE than standing up for what is truth and justice. Esther had to go to the King to save her people. Many of us did as was required and Humbled ourselves and prayed, HE could heal our land, our NATION. WE WENT TO THE POLLS AND VOTED. FAITH WITHOUT WORKS IS NOTHING. NOW WE NEED TO CONTINUE TO PRAY. IT IS NOT A TIME TO STOP. BUT WE NEED TO PRAY MORE THAN EVER. DON'T BACK DOWN, BUT FORGE AHEAD. Margene/ Sunwhisp

Sometimes we have to humble ourselves and ask for help! I think this is one of the hardest things to do! For me anyway! I have cried out, and no one heard me! I kept silent and no one saw my tears. I reached up, and HE said, I have the PLAN! Listen and I will show you the WAY! I am searching for what HE wants me to do! What I display on my pages is Me! It is who I am. I need to be the same on here as I am in my own Home as I am in Church, as I am in Public. If I am not, I would be a Hypocrite! He has known me before the Foundations of the World! Before I was formed in my Mommy's Womb. Search ME. He tells us and I will tell you the truth! Love is here. Reach out and grab it. Margene/Sunwhisp ♥

Father, This Prayer Is for Your Children
That Sat upon My Knee...

Father, This prayer is for your Children that sat upon my knee crying upon my shoulder, asking what shall come of me. My heart is so troubled 'cause I do not know what to do this or that is happening, and it only seems to be getting worse. I am losing hope and sinking. It is so out of control.

So, Father, I ask for YOUR direction in all that is to be done. For I am just a person, just a mere Woman. I can't bear their suffering for I do not have the answers that they want to hear.

All I can tell them is to go and to crawl upon YOUR knee and cry upon YOUR Shoulder. Because YOU are their FATHER that knows what to do. 'Cause it is not a surprise to learn what they are going Through. YOU have been waiting for them to come to YOU and ask them what to do. YOU are the one that has the Solution.

So I ask all of YOUR Children that have come to me with tears streaming down their Cheeks. Cry out to JESUS. HE knows what to do. 'Cause I am a mere Woman, not knowing what to do.

I pray that this all makes sense, and it helps even one. I Pray it to My Father and Holy Spirit and number one SON JESUS to help us all to OVERCOME.

In JESUS CHRIST'S precious name. Amen and Amen. Love always, Margene ♥ Margene Wiese-Baier 2012 All prayers will be going into my next book. Thank you. These were inspired by real people that have real needs that have come to me, but I do not have any answers, but to CRY out to JESUS. MWB

Englewood, Florida, beach sunset. Photo by Margene Wiese-Baier © 2012

I am Humbled and so blessed by many of you that have continued to show me Love and respect. God has shown me much about myself. If you ask, HE shows us who we really are. HE has brought many things back to my Memory about my life. The good and the bad. The people that I have loved more than they loved me. The people that didn't love themselves enough to know how much God loved them. HE has shown me the Prophesies that have yet to be fulfilled. HE has brought back the words that HE gave me that no one else had been told. Even the things that HE gave others, but they would not give me because they just could not see me as what God was showing them. I am finding the best Prophesies is from people you don't know. Like Jesus's family and people in his own hometown did not accept who HE was. I want to encourage everyone that has a word from the Lord. Even though it has not come to pass yet. I say YET, because GOD is a Promise Keeper. Keep believing. It is an exciting day we live in. Tonight, I will listen to the recording below. I believe Abba Father is speaking. Quiet yourself and Listen. HE is waiting to speak to you. Love is the Answer. Speak it loudly. Many need to hear you. Most of all, for you to demonstrate it. Hugs. Margene Wiese-Baier 2017

Taking Back What the Enemy Stole
© 2015

Words that Christians used way before the Leviathan snake took them to and Counterfeits them, and then people do not want to use them anymore because they are afraid that they will be looked at as new-agers or worse. Let's take back what belongs to us. Including the Music and the Words that once were so powerful for the KINGDOM of GOD. God is on the Throne, not the devil. He tried that once remember and got thrown out of Heaven. You know who wins. Hallelujah! Love, Margene

FATHER, YOU ARE THE ONE WE WANT TO HONOR BY THE WORDS WE SAY. NOT THE devil! YOUR KINGDOM COME, YOUR WILL BE DONE. WE WANT TO KEEP THE LANGUAGE YOU GAVE US TO MAGNIFY YOU, NOT THE WORLD'S VERSION OF WHAT THE WORDS AND MUSIC AND ALL THAT IS YOURS, WE WANT TO GIVE BACK TO YOU. YOU ARE OUR ROCK AND TRUE SALVATION, NOT TO BE DISTORTED INTO SOMETHING THAT DOES NOT BRING YOU GLORY. FATHER, WE WANT TO LOVE ONLY YOU. FORGIVE US WHEN WE TRY TO SEEK OTHER THINGS THAT WILL ONLY SATISFY OUR FLESH AND CONTAMINATE OUR SOULS. PLEASE FORGIVE THOSE AROUND US THAT ONLY SEEK TO USE US AND THEN THROW US AWAY WHEN THEY HAVE NOT RECEIVED FROM US WHAT THEY WANT. LOVE TO THOSE THAT SEE US THE WAY YOU SEE US. FOR YOU TRULY WILL BLESS THEM. ENCOURAGE THE BROKEN-

HEARTED FOR YOU KNEW THEM BEFORE THE FOUNDATIONS OF THE WORLD BEFORE THEY WERE IN THEIR MOTHER'S WOMB. YOU HAVE A DESTINY AND PLAN FOR THEM. DO NOT LET THEM ABORT THE PLANS YOU HAVE FOR THEM. MAKE THEM STRONG TO WITHHOLD AND PUT DOWN THE WORDS THAT THE ENEMY TRIES TO PUT IN THEIR MINDS OF DESTRUCTION. FOR he is OUT TO KILL, STEAL, AND DESTROY, BUT YOU ARE HERE TO MAGNIFY WHAT YOU PUT INTO THEM. LET THEM SEEK YOU NOW FOR YOU HAVE SOMETHING PERSONAL

Walking it Alone! We May at times feel we are walking alone, but we are never alone because we always have Jesus walking at our side! Margene Wiese-Baier

PS: HE lives in us, so we are NEVER Alone.

Addictions Can Ruin Relationships!

With the State of the World today, finding that Sex Trafficking is an epidemic. The thing that we need to also address is Pornography and addictions that harm relationships. Even Alcohol and Drugs take away people desires for a wholesome relationship with another person. A Man that only had eyes for the Woman in his life all of a sudden is neglecting her needs for Affection because he is gratifying his own needs through Magazines or the internet or even going to sex shops. This is not my usual way to go with my topics that I speak about. But it has been brought more to my attention because of the different Ministries that I have been involved with. And talking to women along the way that have had problems with the men in their lives or have problems themselves. It is very sad hearing women wanting so much to be loved by a man and actually getting into a relationship and married to find out that he would rather be with a woman that is not even there physically.

I have also talked to women that want to be with several partners because that makes them feel wanted. I think that is a Daddy issue. Not feeling loved by their Dad, so they are looking all in the wrong places.

I am learning that Ministries that get involved with Sex Trafficking need to really pray over each other that the enemy does not attack them into Porn!

These Addictions are forms of Adultery! Also, leading to Abuse and Neglect.

I think before getting involved with someone, You need to ask them if they have any addictions. And that they need to be honest about it. Have they repented and conquered it or them?

Some of you have been waiting a long time for your Soul Mate. You don't need or want to be surprised that they would rather stay up all night on the internet while you are in your bed crying 'cause you are all alone. More Alone with someone than when you were single.

A Husband is called to love his wife as Christ Loves the Church! How can a woman respect a man if he is into something that God despises? A Woman needs love and nurturing. In return, he will be treated with Respect and treated like a King in his house.

Leaving on a Happier Note. With Jesus, all can be healed when you turn it all over to HIM. In Jesus. Love, Margene Wiese-Baier

Close your eyes and wrap your arms around yourself tightly and think of how it is when the Father gives you a hug. We need to appreciate who we are. We were made to LOVE, and we need to start with ourselves in order to love other, so give yourself a hug and acknowledge that you are the KING'S KIDS, and after you have done that, spread that love. We would be a happier and healthier World if we would begin to love each other like our *FATHER* loves us. *LOOK* in the Mirror and see *HIS* reflection shining back. Be sparklin'. Remember, a Diamond isn't shiny or sparklin' until all the roughness is chipped or cut away bringing out new facets that reflect the *LIGHT*. Our *LIGHT* is *JESUS*, *Yahweh*! *Margene/Sunwhisp* © 2012

I heard someone say at Church, I feel like Marching. Do you ever feel like Marching? Do you ever feel like you want to Dance or Sing? Do you ever feel that unction in your Gut that if you don't do something, you are going to combust? Do you sometimes feel foolish in doing some things that you just know are from *GOD*, but you also feel a tug pulling you back from being obedient? Are you worried more about what others will think about you than what your Father thinks about you? I know there are times when *HE* has given me a word for someone, and I have a little argument with *HIM*. God, that sounds so unusual. I don't even know. Then I remember the time I was at my friend's Church service, Allen and Francine Fosdick, and we all praying and Prophesying and God gave me the word Eagle, and then the Holy Spirit pushed me again to go tell the man we were praying for, and he told me that was the name of something they were doing in their Ministry. I would have felt bad if I did not say anything, and God gave it to someone else. I have had that happen to me too.

Take the chance! It might not make any sense to you or anyone then, but later they may think about what you said and, voila, clarity. We do not have to please man, but how pleasing it is to Our Father when we open our mouths and let *HIM* speak through it.

Angels in Flight III

Contents

Beautiful!

Colors, Colors, Colors everywhere.

The Waters flow from every stream into river, then the vast oceans. Water trickles down the Mountains. Clean and cool and oh so Clear, vibrant and energizing, invigorating. My Spirit Soars as the water pours over me from the waterfall set in the pool of LIFE.

I feel Courage as the words of HIS love are spoken to me. Telling me to come closer. I am mesmerized by HIS Beauty. Sparkling and Translucent like Gold through the Water. I am YOURS and YOU are Mine for all time. Margene/Sunwhisp ♥

Photo taken by Margene Wiese-Baier

When God Calls You to Do Something

When God calls you to do something, you can take a step of Faith and see where God takes you. Or you can stay where you're at and wonder What if for the rest of your Life. Like Jonah and the Whale. He let fear overtake him, and he got on a boat, and he tried to hide from God in where HE wanted Him to go, and look what happened to him. He got thrown overboard. He got swallowed by a Whale and had to cry out to God. And he had to ask for forgiveness. Got Slimed and Spit out and then went where he was supposed to go in the first place.

When you are sold out to God, and HE asks you to go someplace. Please be obedient. You will be glad that you did.
Pastor Margene Wiese-Baier
5/15/2015https://www.biblegateway.com/passage/?search=Jonah+1

Venice Beach

They Say Love Is Where the Heart Is!

They say Love is where the Heart is! I have been on a Journey for a while now. I first went to Florida from Oregon because I wanted to not be tempted to go back into a relationship. Not because I hated that person, but because I know women and how they will go back time and time again into a relationship they should flee from. I did not want to come back to Oregon until I knew I would not be tempted. I have been back a few times now and left thinking I would not want to move back.

On my Journey, I have been to several locations. I went to Florida for fifteen years, Pennsylvania, and Georgia and now back in Oregon. Loving each place in different ways.

I feel I am being led by the Holy Spirit and being obedient to HIS calling on my life. Remembering what Pastor Freda King told me Go where you are Celebrated and not just Tolerated. The thing is that we are put in certain families for a reason. We may not know that reason until God brings us full circle back to where we started. God's timing is everything. There was lot to learn before HE brought me back. The one thing I know is that my Daddy is a very special man and truly hungers and thirsts for the Word of God. He wants to listen to me when I talk about Jesus. He loves his children and wants the best for them. God has placed in him a loving and compassionate heart for others. He has been a caregiver to many. Now it is His children's turn to give back to him.

So home is where the HEART is; for now, that place is back where I began. Oregon, the place I grew up, the place I had my little family, the place I call home. I will go where God leads me. Unfortunately, we don't always appreciate those that we hold dearest in our hearts until God brings us full circle. Truly healing from our past will make us confront things that we thought we dealt with long ago. We have a loving compassionate God that will not only heal your heart but heal those that we not only meet along the way but those that we have carried with us.

Please pray for your families. He might bring you back to help you heal but go to HIM and ask what you need to do to Move Forward in your life. Most of all, find JOY in all that you do.

Love is always the Answer, for GOD IS LOVE and LOVE IS GOD!

Learn to Love again. Forgive the ones that hurt you. Remember hurt people hurt people. Allow them to move forward. It is time. Release them and you release yourself. Allowing the doors to open to your DESTINY.

WHAT BIBLE VERSES DO YOU SEE THAT GOES WITH THIS? LOVE, Margene/Sunwhisp

I Don't Want to Live in Fear

I do not want to be in fear, but I do not want to hide my head in the sand and not know when I need to be in prayer. I can look back in my life and see where God sent HIS Angels to protect me. When I felt someone touch my shoulder and my cousin yelled at me to stop when policemen were chasing us when we were on the way home from a friend's house. If I would not have stopped, I would have been shot in the back. They were after someone that had been robbing houses in the neighborhood. Since it was late at night, we were suspect, and crossing an empty field made it even more likely that we were guilty. But I turned around, and we were able to prove our innocence.

Another time when a car drove right in front of me and I stopped just in time not to hit them. Only had a human's width between their car and mine. Wow, we both were at a standstill. Only had time to say Oh God; the other person looked at me and then drove off. I was shaken up but was able to drive off. Thanking HIM for not allowing an accident to happen.

And then the time I was at a cross walk about to cross and felt a hand again on my shoulder and I think hearing a voice say stop. Just before a car came so close to where I was standing.

Of course, the time I could have died instantly when I caught my shoe in the crack of a sidewalk and fell flat on my face, and as I was flying through the air saying to God if you are ready for me to come HOME, I am ready, but if you still have work for me to do, I am willing to stay. Wow, some days, I wish HE would have just taken me Home. It has not been easy being here, and the things I have gone through since that day. I hate getting hurt and would not wish that on anyone. I pray that I am passing every test HE places before me. One thing I will tell you: when you think that you are going to die, you are not thinking about wow, I am not married or thinking about yourself. You are wanting to make sure you pleased HIM. My concern was if I finished what I was sent to earth to do. Jeremiah 29:11. Knowing that HE knew us before the Foundation of the World and that I said yes to my Assignment. I now think of that a lot.

There are many other stories of where God intervened in my life to prevent me not only from being physically hurt, but also getting in the wrong relationships.

He gave me a warning dream about 9/11. Another about the China Wall coming down. But who am I that anyone would listen at that time? We did not have Facebook to share our dreams and visions, and if you are not recognized in the World as a Prophet or a Person that has dreams and visions, all you can do is pray about the things that God shows you.

I don't like to get hurt or go into the Hospital and would rather have not had these things happen to me, but I have learned that GOD is my

Protector and Provision and will use certain things to teach us and give us Wisdom to help others. Without these things I would not have a testimony of how HE brought me through.

You may ask what does all of this have to do with what I started this story with. It just shows that God is with us and that HE sends us HIS Angels to protect us, but if we do not listen to HIS warnings, we will be caught up in the distractions of life and not see what is right in front of us that we need to PRAY about.

I know a lot of you have had similar stories to tell that is your testimony. All I know is God can use everything that we went through to bring us through that not only helps us grow, but to help others, so they won't have to go through things if they are willing to listen. This life was not meant for us to live in torment, but to give us life more abundantly. He allows certain things to draw us closer to HIM. We are not victims, but VICTORIOUS. LET US SHOUT HALLELUJAH! GOD BLESS ALL OF YOU READING THIS AND GIVE HIM ALL OF THE GLORY. LET US ALWAYS PRAY IN JESUS'S HOLY NAME. AMEN AND AMEN!

WE ARE NOW IN A TIME OF OUR LIVES. WE BETTER BE CLEAR WHO OR IS IT WHOM WE ARE GOING TO FOLLOW. LET IT BE HIM. YAHWEH. YESHUA, KING OF KINGS, BRIGHT AND MORNING STAR. GET OUT THE SHOFAR AND BLOW IT FOR ALL TO HEAR. HALLELUJAH!

My Heart Is Broken

My Heart is breaking on a personal level, but also on a Global level as I see all the terrible things that is happening. The Heartless people in our Government. The wreckless people that would rather have their way than protect our Country. The hatred toward our President is real and not imagined. It is truly disgraceful what is going on in a Country that many would love to be part of in legal ways. Yes, my Heart is breaking. It is a deep sense of Sadness. I feel HIM weeping with me. It is time that we come together for HIM and let HIM heal our lands. Protect our Land Love, Margene

Time to Pray

Many of us have things that are going on in our lives that only Praying to Abba Father in Jesus's Name can fix. It is time to Pray, Pray, Pray. We need repentance in all things that we have let get by us that has cost us Love and understanding for others. I believe Abba Father is redirecting us back to HIM. For all things of evil can be turned back to Good. Yes, the devil is a liar, and we need to remind him that he has no power over us in Jesus's name, but he is a defeated foe, him and his cohorts. He is an itty bitty devil and we have a very big God. (I don't know who first said that, but I like it so I will use it) Come on now. WHO HAS THE POWER! We have in us the truth of all, and HIS name is JESUS, YESHUA. HALLELUJAH! THE MOST HIGH GOD! Love, Margene 📷💗

Forgiveness

At this time of year, I think of people that I need to Forgive. Not wanting to bring the hurt that they caused me into the next year. Not waiting to Forgive them until they come to me and ask for Forgiveness, but forgiving them either way. Not letting them off the hook per se but giving myself the Freedom to pursue the things that I need to go on with my Life. For the rest of December, I want to feel Happy and content and in the knowledge that no one else has control over how I feel. No more feeling hurt, but my goal is to feel HAPPY AND JOY in the Season that we celebrate in the Love of JESUS!

I am finding that I do not want to burn BRIDGES with people but keep the connections open. I find that I may need that person again in my life or even better they may need me again. And then there are some that it is best to just leave the door closed. Allowing the Abba Father to heal me completely.

I long for Friendships and Love to be a Lifetime or even for all Eternity but have come to a realization some relationships are just meant to be short term. Some we just learn what we do not want in our lives. Some we learn how we truly want to be treated, and some we learn a lesson that will bring us even Closer to Jesus

I long for those relationships that do bring me closer to Jesus. I long for those people to come into my life that HE has destined me to be with that will bring others into the Fold of Jesus's Kingdom.

More than that Forgiveness is Freedom from the Past to go into the Future. This year is almost over, but enough time to change the OUTLOOK for the New Year.

I pray all of you to have a Wonderful Christmas and a Spectacular New Year! Full of Wisdom and Happiness, Success, and Prosperity.

Most of all, Forgive one another, but if you need to Forgive yourself, Do so. Allow HIM to Clean your Heart for a Fresh Start. Love, Margene Wiese-Baier. Sunwhisp 12/17/2018

A Peculiar Person!

I have loved Jesus since I was a little girl. My Mom taught me about HIM; sometimes I think she was telling me about HIM while I was in her womb. And to learn that HE knew me before the foundations of the World and before I was formed in my Mother's womb, I am sure of it. I am not saying I was ever perfect, but as a child, I felt I belonged more in Heaven than on earth. Maybe that seems strange to some of you. Okay, maybe even weird, but we are called a peculiar people for a reason. Some days seemed more like a dream than reality. I loved the Father, Son, and Holy Spirit so much that I would go out and sing to them at the top of my Lungs. Even after I had my tonsils out, I could not stop from going outside and sing to HIM. I was told not to but had too. Then I would have to sing at night to HIM before I could go to sleep. I find myself even today waking up and singing to HIM. I always prayed, "FATHER, NEVER LET ME GO AWAY FROM YOU!" I DON'T EVER WANT TO LOSE MY LOVE FOR HIM. HE IS MY ALL AND ALL MY EVERYTHING! I told my daughters about HIM even in the Womb. I was the one that always made sure we went to Church, so they would learn even more.

I grew up a Lutheran and remember going to Church with a couple that was my Dad's foster parents. A lovely couple. My brothers and I stayed with them probably for the weekend. I am not clear on that, but I do remember the Church they went to. It seemed all the women were crying, and I asked Mrs. Miller why they were crying, and she said they were crying for happiness. As a little girl that satisfied me, and I went on my way being happy to know they were happy.

My main thing is I love HIM with all of my HEART and my MIND is made up that HE is the one and only GOD, and JESUS is the ONE and ONLY way to go to HEAVEN. I won't argue with you about it, but I will tell you about HIM. I am only to plant the seed and let the HOLY SPIRIT take care of the rest. So I know HE still speaks today. And I know HE speaks to everyone differently, so if you want to hear from HIM, get quiet and ask HIM to tell you something. Read the word. Listening is more important than telling HIM all your problems. And thank HIM for all that HE has already done. OK, I know HE is waiting to hear from YOU. Love, Margene

Do Not Lose Your CONFIDENCE!

Do not lose your Confidence. Think about it: where does the enemy attack you the most? In your mind. If he can make you feel like you can't do something, then he has made headway. Excuse the Pun. The devil is a liar. He is out to steal, kill, and destroy. You may think he is out to kill you physically, but that would not be advantages to him. You know why, because he knows that you would go to Heaven. And he certainly does not want that. So he wants to mess you up Emotionally so you won't be able to serve the KING. Come on, this is real. No fooling around anymore. 2020 is the year for PROMOTION and ACCELERATION. The things that you have been trying to get done, achieve for months or even years you are going to get done in days, and weeks. The time is now. No, more sitting on projects. God is clearing up your mind and showing you how to do things that people have been telling you that they are too hard for you to do. Or worse yet you were telling yourself. Hooplah! Get ready, get ready, get ready. I know this is for me, but who else is it for. God did not show me, but if this is for you. Please let me know. It is important when someone posts something and you read it, you let them know.
Margene Wiese-Baier

Taking Back What the Enemy Stole

Words that Christians used way before the Leviathan snake took them to and counterfeits them and then people do not want to use them anymore because they are afraid that they will be looked at as new agers or worse. Let's take back what belongs to us. Including the Music and the Words that once were so powerful for the KINGDOM of GOD. God is on the Throne, not the devil. He tried that once remember and got thrown out of Heaven. You know who wins. Hallelujah! Love, Margene

FATHER, YOU ARE THE ONE WE WANT TO HONOR BY THE WORDS WE SAY. NOT THE devil! YOUR KINGDOM COME, YOUR WILL BE DONE. WE WANT TO KEEP THE LANGUAGE YOU GAVE US TO MAGNIFY YOU, NOT THE WORLD'S VERSION OF WHAT THE WORDS AND MUSIC AND ALL THAT IS YOURS, WE WANT TO GIVE BACK TO YOU. YOU ARE OUR ROCK AND TRUE SALVATION. NOT TO BE DISTORTED INTO SOMETHING THAT DOES NOT BRING YOU GLORY. FATHER, WE WANT TO LOVE ONLY YOU. FORGIVE US WHEN WE TRY TO SEEK OTHER THINGS THAT WILL ONLY SATISFY OUR FLESH AND CONTAMINATE OUR SOULS. PLEASE FORGIVE THOSE AROUND US THAT ONLY SEEK TO USE US AND THEN THROW US AWAY WHEN THEY HAVE NOT RECEIVED FROM US WHAT THEY WANT. LOVE TO THOSE THAT SEE US THE WAY YOU SEE US. FOR YOU TRULY WILL BLESS THEM. ENCOURAGE THE BROKEN HEARTED FOR YOU KNEW THEM BEFORE THE FOUNDATIONS

OF THE WORLD BEFORE THEY WERE IN THEIR MOTHER'S WOMB. YOU HAVE A DESTINY AND PLAN FOR THEM. DO NOT LET THEM ABORT THE PLANS YOU HAVE FOR THEM. MAKE THEM STRONG TO WITHHOLD AND PUT DOWN THE WORDS THAT THE ENEMY TRIES TO PUT IN THEIR MINDS OF DESTRUCTION. FOR he is OUT TO KILL, STEAL, AND DESTROY, BUT YOU ARE HERE TO MAGNIFY WHAT YOU PUT INTO THEM. LET THEM SEEK YOU NOW FOR YOU HAVE SOMETHING PERSONAL TO SAY TO THEM. SHOW OUR CHILDREN AND GRANDCHILDREN THAT YOU HAVE A PLAN FOR THEM, AND WE PRAY BLESSINGS OVER THEM. WE ARE CALLED TO BE PRIESTS AND KINGS AS PROPHET NWAKA SPOKE AT THE CMFI CONFERENCE. PROPHET BENJAMIN SPOKE LIFE BACK INTO AMERICA. WE NEED TO REACH ALL OF THE NATIONS OF THE WORLD AND NOT WATER DOWN THE TRUTH AS PROPHET BENJAMIN SPOKE.

COME ON, WAKE UP, NOT ONLY AMERICA, BUT THE WORLD, FOR OUR KING IS GOOD. FATHER, WE ASK ALL OF THESE THINGS IN THE LORD JESUS CHRIST'S NAME, AMEN AND AMEN. HALLELUJAH! LOVE, MARGENE ♥

Please write something that we need to get back and put in its rightful place as Christians. Believers in the LORD JESUS CHRIST! AMEN. HALLELUJAH! JESUAH REIGNS! YAWEH! KING OF KINGS!

Seizing the Moment

Seizing the Moment. How many times have you passed up an opportunity just because you let fear of the unknown stop you. I know I have. It is time to seize the MOMENT and take that STEP OF FAITH! What's is the worse thing that can HAPPEN? You may have to regroup and take a STEP in a different direction. At least you were OPEN to see what GOD has for you. I say I love change, but that doesn't always mean I am totally happy about it. Sometimes it is downright scary, but I have found I am pretty adaptable. I go where GOD leads me. And have been happily surprised with some of the things HE comes up with. I would never think of some of the things that HE does. But HE listens to my concern, and it is amazing that the thing I am concerned about HE already has it all worked out. You know why? 'Cause HE has already went before me. I LOVE YOU, LORD. I will sing YOU PRAISES. I WILL DANCE BEFORE My AUDIENCE OF ONE. I will lift my HANDS and ADORE YOU. OPEN MY EYES TO SEE ALL THE OPPORTUNITIES YOU SET BEFORE ME. HELP me. HEAR YOUR VOICE ONLY. HELP me to not only take a STEP OF FAITH. BUT TO LEAP INTO WHAT YOU HAVE FOR me. YUP! I AM READY TO SEE WHAT YOU HAVE FOR me 'cause I know that whatever it is, it is GOOD. Love, Margene Wiese-Baier

Breaking Free for Your Victory...

He thought it was a game that you were willing to play. He chased all the little girls in grade School and they would giggle and laugh when he caught them. Then he would let them go and go on to chase another. So when he saw you, he thought you would love to be chased too. He wasn't that good looking, but it was so cute how he just kept pursuing you. Everyone kept telling you how beautiful you were and that you could have any guy you wanted, but they were just looking and he was chasing, making you feel like you were beautiful. He told you so. He started out loving and kind. He told you that he would love you just the way you were. He talked to you about everything. At first, you felt safe. You felt free to use your talents. He was even encouraging at first. He wanted you with him everywhere he went. He started to make excuses. He would even make plans with you to change them at the last minute. He pushed you until you became angry. That gave him the excuse he needed to go to his friends. Holidays were the worst; he caused a fight, so you would just throw up your arms and just say, "Don't bother getting me anything." Even though you just bought him something that he has been wanting for a long time.

What happened? Did he change or were you just growing into what God wanted you to become and he didn't like it. At first you woke up happy, but he woke up a Grump. He stopped wanting to take you everywhere. He just seemed to stop caring. You feeling sucked dry. But GOD reached out. HE sent people your way that helped you see the truth. Your JOY was being slowly or fading away. A distant memory of actually feeling happy to be alive was drifting in to the abyss. Nothing but a fog was growing over your eyes, and you could no longer see that you wanted to be loved by this man.

Women, you hate to admit it, but some men just have an ULTERIOR MOTIVE, and they will put up with you until you WAKE UP and see their ploy. You wanted Love, and they just wanted whatever you had to give.

When you look back, don't look at the good times that you had that will only give a way for the enemy to toy with your mind and when that silver-tongued devil comes back and sweet talks you, you will fall into his trap again. Counteract by remembering how he yelled at you. How he left you home while he went off and was with his friends. Remember how much money you spent on him. How you gave up your independence to support him in what he wanted to do.

Couples are to complement each other, to support each other, to encourage. Not have an ULTERIOR MOTIVE to take the other for all they have.

I am glad I had my Faith in a FATHER THAT LOVES ME that brought me to realize I am worth more. THAT HE HAS A PLAN FOR MY LIFE. JEREMIAH 29:11

I am thankful for the people that HE sent me to tell me the truth about the men that were out to take advantage.

THIS IS NOT JUST MY STORY, BUT FOR MANY WOMEN OUT THERE. ONCE WE GET THAT WE ARE THE KING'S LITTLE PRINCESSES AND WOE BE TO THE MEN THAT TRY TO HURT US. BEING THANKFUL THAT HE HAS GIVEN US AN ESCAPE ROUTE. HE OPENED THE DOOR. NOW WALK THROUGH IT AND CLOSE IT TIGHTLY. DON'T GO BACK. ONLY REASON TO REMEMBER IS TO TELL OTHER'S YOUR TESTIMONY, AND HOW GOOD GOD IS FOR RESCUING YOU. WHEN AN EAGLE PUSHES HER EAGLET OUT OF THE NEST, THEY CAN EITHER SOAR TO NEW HEIGHTS OR IF THEY START TO FALL, SHE GOES UNDER THEM AND CATCHES THEM. EITHER WAY, SHE HAS PROTECTED THEM. LIKE YOUR LOVING FATHER.

IF YOU HAVEN'T DONE IT YET, TAKE THE STEP TO YOUR FREEDOM. GET YOUR JOY BACK. NO MAN IS WORTH LOSING WHAT GOD HAS FOR YOU. THEY SHOULD BE THE ONES BRINGING YOU CLOSER TO WHERE GOD WANTS YOU, NOT TRYING TO TAKE YOU THE OTHER DIRECTION.

WE ARE CALLED TO BE VICTORIOUS, NOT VICTIMS.

IF YOU CAN'T DO IT ALONE, FIND SOMEONE TO HELP YOU. I AM THANKFUL FOR FRIENDS THAT LOVE US ENOUGH TO TELL

US THE TRUTH. IT IS HARD TO HEAR SOMETIMES, BUT IF YOU ARE TRUTHFUL, GOD WAS

New Living Translation
The tongue can bring death or life; those who love to talk will reap the consequences.

LOVE, Margene Wiese-Baier

Sweet Little Boy Healed! To the Glory of God!

When I was in Honduras, this was in 2005, the job that I was given was to pray for the people. It was a Medical Mission Trip. The people would go see the Medical team first and then would come to me and I would pray for them. For some reason, the Woman that was also supposed to pray for them just had me pray for them. But she would bring the people into the room. She carried this little boy over to me that looked like he was dying. He was so weak, I had to hold him on my lap a certain way 'cause he could not sit on my lap. I closed my eyes and started singing in the Spirit. There was an older woman that was dancing in front of me Praying and Dancing. I had Honduran Women Assistants. I seemed to be praying over him for a long time. And then I opened my eyes and looked at this beautiful little boy, and he had opened his eyes and looked at me. Remember he was so weak and lifeless. I said to him LOCO INSPIRIT O (about the Woman dancing) and he said LOCO. Then we smiled at each other. In that instance, he was healed. That older Woman was beautiful, and I called her a Momma-Sieta. My friend came over and said, "Margene, I am going to take him back to the Doctors." She took him back to document and to show them he was healed. Then she brought him back and told me she was going to give him some bread. Remember the little boy that was carried in and put in my arms walked to see the Doctors. Hallelujah! Margene

Photo in Honduras, Photo, Margene Wiese-Baier

GOD, not Buddha. Our *FATHER* with One Son *JESUS CHRIST* and *THE HOLY SPIRIT. WE HAVE THE KE. LET US USE IT. PRAYING!* LOVE, Margene

Acts 13:21 ▶
Parallel Verses
New International Version
Then the people asked for a king, and he gave them Saul son of Kish, of the tribe of Benjamin, who ruled forty years.

New Living Translation
Then the people begged for a king, and God gave them Saul son of Kish, a man of the tribe of Benjamin, who reigned for forty years.

Acts 13:22 ▶
Parallel Verses
New International Version
After removing Saul, he made David their king. God testified concerning him: "I have found David son of Jesse, a man after my own heart; he will do everything I want him to do."

New Living Translation
But God removed Saul and replaced him with David, a man about whom God said, "I have found David son of Jesse, a man after my own heart. He will do everything I want him to do."

Turning Over a New Leaf!

One thing that I have been thinking about, that has been on my mind is that the Rainbow should not represent the Gay population, but the many colors of People that represent our World. God's Creation. I wrote a song about the Love that we should have for each other. And the truth is that if we are cut, we all bleed red.

This Christmas, I would like everyone to forget that they dislike someone because of their color, but to embrace them and know beyond knowing that God is not going to put us in different sections.

Do you ever imagine what Heaven will be like? I do! OH my, the person that may have lived in a Shack on earth may have a bigger Mansion than the one that had a Mansion on earth.

How can you make this a better World? It may be just a smile, a hug, a sandwich, a cup of water. What if you started today just speaking a kind word to that person that you have been avoiding just because they don't look like you. Actually! I have to admit that there are some women of color that are more beautiful to me. For you see, when God made us, HE wanted us all to be Unique and beautiful. But HE didn't take one mold but created many. And HE brought out HIS Paint Pallet and said, "I painted a white baby a little while ago. Let me paint this child a soft Chocolate color, with dark brown eyes or maybe even blue, because the Daddy has blue eyes because he fell in love with a dark-eyed beauty with the skin color of ebony."

I love the way GOD interacts in our lives to bring people together. We need to get over that we need to Marry within our own race or color. It amazes me when reading the Bible that HE brought us together through these things that some put their nose up at. So the next time you see a Japanese person with a sugar-white person, rejoice; the next you see an Indian person with a white person. Know this: God brought them together for a reason. And that reason is HE had a Divine Purpose and a Plan for them to impact the World. HE is still going to bring the same races together. And that amazes me to that they may not have met in their own Country, but after coming to America, HE brings them together.

So as I said the Rainbow should represent the PEOPLE that Abba Father made to inhabit the World. Appreciate who HE made you to be. And seek HIM to see what HE would want you to be. For it is Good. Remember the enemy is out to Kill, Steal, and Destroy. You can't allow the itty bitty devil to mess with you or you can allow Our Father to bring you into fulfill what HIS plan is for you.

I chose to LOVE all colors of the Rainbow. The colors of the People of the World.

And by the way we need to stop Stereotyping people for what a few do. In every nationality, there are good people and bad. Let us see people how Jesus sees them.

Love, Margene Wiese-Baier Christmas Eve

Looking forward to a great New Year, but want to go out with a Bang this year! A Love bang! Shalom! Peace, be Still!

My Mom's Birthday

It would be my Mom's birthday today. I cannot believe she has been in Heaven since 1985. She was our Mother, Mom, Ma, but oh so much more. She was our friend.
Love, Margene c/o 2016

Ask for Wisdom!

The Bible says, "If any of you lacks wisdom, let him ASK of God, who gives" (James 1:5). Because we can't receive what we ask for, we believe that it has never been given, when in fact, it has. So our receiving or rather our inability to receive is based on our soul being tied to someone. In other words, we receive from the person with whom we have soul-ties. A soul-tie is a connection of the heart (See Hebrews 4:12). There are good soul-ties and bad soul-ties. There are soul-ties that produce life in us, and there are soul-ties that produce death in us. God wants us to break the soul-ties that produce death. Check Sunwhisp's Marriage and Single pages for more information.

Don't Stop PRAYING!

It is definitely not time to quit Praying, but to Pray to still the voices of the Snakes and deceivers the enemy has unleashed. He is angry that Our choice, God's choice, is not his choice. Now before my family and friends that wanted Hillary gets theirs in a bunch, I want to make it clear I am talking about the people that are in Authority to cause division. It does cause me great sadness that personal friends and family have been divided over this election, and it is time for all of us to put this behind us and work together to help bring this Great Nation back to being Great again. As you know, we are held to a Higher standard than the rest of the World. Praying for Peace and reconciliation. Praying that Trump stands up and does what he has promised to do and does not sway from them. Knowing how to Hear God's voice. Praying Abba Father has great influence on him. A Holy Spirit baptism. More Clarity, Great Wisdom, and surrounding himself with godly men as Trump learns. I do pray that Ben Carson reconsiders and continues to stand in the gap for him. Using his strengths and learning from his weaknesses that others will know how to do those things.

Yes, there is still much to pray for above all, to shut the bad lion's mouth and to Let Our KING LION Roar, the LION OF JUDAH, BRINGING OUR NATION UP AND OUT FOR GREATNESS, NOT ONLY FOR AMERICANS BUT TO HELP LEAD THE WAY of Healing. IN JESUS'S NAME. LOVE, Margene

About Angels in Flight

Angels in Flight was born out of knowing that I had angels all around me. My mom from a young age taught me about Jesus and that I had a Guardian Angel to protect me. She taught my brothers, sister, and I the prayer that she wrote.

Now I lay me down to sleep
Angels guard my little nest Glad and well may I wake
I ask it all for Jesus's sake

Everything in this book is inspired by the Holy Spirit.
May it be a blessing to each person that reads it.

Love in Jesus,

Margene

About the Author

Margene Wiese-Baier was born as Margene Annette Wiese. Born to Curtis Allen Wiese and Margaret Ann Wicklund-Wiese on October 29, 1951. Margene has two brothers and a sister. She also has two living daughters and one in Heaven. She grew up in Oregon and later moved to Florida and several places. Was inspired by Bill Cameron to be a missionary to Honduras and India. She also developed many pages on Facebook which all were dedicated to Abba Father, Jesus, and Holy Spirit. She is looking forward to her next chapters and her destiny in life.

www.ingramcontent.com/pod-product-compliance
Lightning Source LLC
Chambersburg PA
CBHW041113120626
46547CB00019B/2687